1994

D0469215

Canadian Biography Series

MICHAEL ONDAATJE:
EXPRESS YOURSELF BEAUTIFULLY

Express yourself beautifully.

Michael Ondaatje in London, Ontario, circa 1969.

1994

Michael Ondaatje

EXPRESS YOURSELF BEAUTIFULLY

Ed Jewinski

ECW PRESS

CANADIAN CATALOGUING IN PUBLICATION DATA

Jewinski, Ed, 1948–
Michael Ondaatje : express yourself beautifully

Includes bibliographical references.

ISBN 1-55022-189-2

1. Ondaatje, Michael, 1943– – Biography. 2. Poets, Canadian
(English) – 20th century – Biography.* 1. Title.

PS8529.N283Z7 1994   C811'.54   C94-931138-3
PR9199.3.053Z7 1994

This book has been published with the assistance of the Ministry
of Culture, Tourism and Recreation of the Province of Ontario,
through funds provided by the Ontario Publishing Centre, and with
the assistance of grants from the Department of Communications,
The Canada Council, the Ontario Arts Council, and the Government
of Canada through the Canadian Studies and Special Projects
Directorate of the Department of the Secretary of State of Canada.

Design and imaging by ECW Type & Art, Oakville, Ontario.
Printed by Imprimerie Gagné, Louiseville, Québec.

Distributed by General Distribution Services,
30 Lesmill Road, Toronto, Ontario M3B 2T6.
(416) 445-3333, (800) 387-0172 (Canada), FAX (416) 445-5967.

Distributed to the trade in the United States exclusively
by InBook, 140 Commerce Street, P.O. Box 120261,
East Haven, Connecticut, U.S.A. 06512.
(203) 467-4257, FAX (203) 469-8364.
Customer service: (800) 243-0138, FAX (800) 334-3892.

Distributed in the United Kingdom by Drake Marketing,
St. Fagans Road, Fairwater, Cardiff CF5 3AE, (0222) 560333.

Published by ECW PRESS,
2120 Queen Street East, Suite 200
Toronto, Ontario M4E 1E2.

ACKNOWLEDGEMENTS

My thanks go to Kim Ondaatje; the Wilfrid Laurier Research Department for an initiatory grant; and, in alphabetical order, Douglas Barbour, Joanne Buchan, Wayne Clifford, Stan Dragland, Anna M. Grant (Bishop's University archivist), James Hertel, Robert Lecker, Stuart MacKinnon, Tom Marshall, Tony Urquhart, and Mary Williams. Christopher Ondaatje's memoir, *The Man-Eater of Punanai*, has helped me immeasurably. In the works-consulted section I list only those whom I have quoted, but I must also thank all the others whose works I have absorbed and relied on to help me finish this book. Your guidance has helped; any errors and misperceptions are, of course, my fault, not yours.

PHOTOGRAPHS: Cover, Isolde Ohlbaum © Isolde Ohlbaum, München; frontispiece illustration, Kim Ondaatje, is used by permission of the photographer; illustration 2, reprinted from *The Man-Eater of Punanai* by permission of Christopher Ondaatje; illustrations 3, 4, 5, and 10 are used by permission of Bishop's University Archives; illustrations 6 and 18, Steve Behal, are used by permission of the photographer; illustration 7, Brian Toll, is used by permission of the photographer; illustration 8 is used by permission of Elizabeth Whalley; illustration 9 is used by permission of the Sidney Nolan Trust; illustration 11, *London Free Press* Collection of Photographic Negatives, the D.B. Weldon Library, University of Western Ontario, London, Ontario, N6A 3K7; illustration 12, Robert Lansdale, is used by permission of the photographer; illustration 13 is used by permission of Kim Ondaatje; illustration 14, Michel Lambeth, Toronto, is used by permission of the Lambeth family; illustration 15, Jack Chiang, is used by permission of the photographer; illustrations 16 and 21 are used by permission of CANAPRESS; illustration 17, Steve Bosch, is used by permission of the *Vancouver Sun*; illustration 19, J. Goode, is used by permission of the *Toronto Star*; illustration 20, Erik Christensen, is used by permission of the *Globe and Mail*, Toronto; illustration 22, Russell Monk, is used by permission of the photographer; illustration 23 is used by permission of AP/Wide World Photos.

To Hans
and "friendly sibling rivalry"

TABLE OF CONTENTS

ACKNOWLEDGEMENTS   5

LIST OF ILLUSTRATIONS   8

Michael Ondaatje: Express Yourself Beautifully   9

CHRONOLOGY   137

WORKS CONSULTED   140

LIST OF ILLUSTRATIONS

Michael Ondaatje .... *cover*
1. Express yourself beautifully .... *frontispiece*
2. What we think of married life: Doris and Mervyn Ondaatje ... 12
3. Arthur Motyer teaches 26
4. Michael Ondaatje as Billy Budd in *Innocence at Sea* 29
5. Doug Jones at Bishop's University 32
6. Kim Ondaatje 35
7. Michael Ondaatje as a graduate of the University of
   Toronto, 1965 42
8. George Whalley and parrot 48
9. Sidney Nolan (Australia, 1917–1992), *Death of Sergeant Kennedy
   at Stringybark Creek*, 1946, enamel on composition board,
   91.5 × 122.0 cm. Gift of Sunday Reed, 1977, collection of the
   National Gallery of Australia, Canberra 57
10. Michael Ondaatje, cover drawing for *The Mitre* 62
11. Michael Ondaatje in 1971 78
12. Michael Ondaatje participates (with Al Purdy and Diane
    Wakoski) in a University of Toronto poetry workshop 81
13. Blue Roof Farm 86
14. Michael Ondaatje and Wallace in 1974 89
15. Michael Ondaatje 96
16. Michael Ondaatje celebrates winning the Governor General's
    Award for *There's a Trick with a Knife I'm Learning to Do* 103
17. Earle Birney presents the Governor General's Award to
    Michael Ondaatje 104
18. Kim Ondaatje, filmmaker 109
19. Linda Spalding 110
20. Michael Ondaatje in 1979 113
21. Michael Ondaatje edits *Love Clinic* in 1991 117
22. Michael Ondaatje in 1992 121
23. Booker Prize winner Michael Ondaatje 129

Michael Ondaatje

EXPRESS YOURSELF BEAUTIFULLY

PROLOGUE

"A horse once bit me on the left breast," Kim Ondaatje explained
to me, "and the next thing I knew was that Michael claimed that
a camel had bitten off his mother's left breast. I wasn't surprised.
As a writer he absorbed everything — but changed it for his own
needs." One of those needs was to fill an inner gap created by
the sense that he, as a child, needed to compensate for being
"weaned on half a body." In this quote from *The Dainty Monsters*,
Michael Ondaatje is referring to his youth, though indirectly, and
to his separation from his parents. But that allusion is oblique,
and requires some understanding of what happened to his father,
to his mother, to his siblings, and — most importantly — to
Ondaatje himself during his childhood.

THE TEA ESTATE

The Ondaatjes have always named their males Philip. Michael's
full name is Philip Michael Ondaatje; his grandfather's is Philip
Jurgen; his father's is Philip Mervyn; his brother's is Philip Christopher; his own son's is Philip Christopher Griffin Ondaatje.
When or why this family tradition started, no one is quite sure.
I wrote to Michael Ondaatje to ask for his help. In his short reply,
he sympathized with the challenges of a biographer, but confessed that he already felt too vulnerable, too "over-revealed and
dangerously self-conscious."

He feels so self-conscious that he hasn't corrected his *Canadian Who's Who* entry (reprinted from 1969 to 1992), which claims that Michael Ondaatje is responsible for developing and breeding "The Sydenham Spaniel." No such breed of dog exists. To the compilers of an edition of *Contemporary Authors*, Ondaatje gave the wrong day of birth while also claiming to be a recognized "hound breeder and hog breeder." As if that wasn't enough, he left even his best friend, Stan Dragland, puzzled about why he, Ondaatje, would claim to be the inventor of the "Dragland hog feeder." "I've never seen this [*Contemporary Authors*] entry," Stan Dragland wrote, "and if there's a joke involved, I don't get it."

Ondaatje wants to maintain his privacy, but he clearly doesn't want to be forgotten. He rarely offers accurate information about his life, and when pestered by reporters or interviewers he resorts to wit to deflect attention from anything truly personal: How do you feel about winning the Toronto Arts Award? "Does this mean I have amnesty from parking tickets?" Did you know that the Trillium Award provides the publisher with two thousand dollars to advertise your book? "Frankly I think they'll probably use the money for a big party." Will your life change if you win the Booker? "I might take a few more taxis" (see Quill, Currie, and Nickson).

Ondaatje will display his sense of humour — but will not reveal why he needs to use it to protect himself. Even his date and place of birth are difficult to establish, and such facts are usually the easiest for the biographer to nail down. In the biographical information included in his books Ondaatje claims to have been born in Colombo, Ceylon (now called Sri Lanka). His former wife, Kim Ondaatje, assures me that in fact "Michael was born on September 12, 1943, in Kegalle, about fifty miles west of Colombo, Ceylon (Sri Lanka), near the tea estate Christopher Ondaatje describes in his book *The Man-Eater of Punanai*."

Michael Ondaatje was the fourth child born to Enid Doris (née Gratiaen) and Philip Mervyn Ondaatje; his siblings are Christopher, Gillian, and Janet. As Ondaatje wrote in *Running in the Family*, his place of birth, Ceylon, because it produced tea, coffee, rubber, rice, spices, and jewels such as rubies, emeralds, and sapphires

seduced all of Europe. The Portuguese. The Dutch. The English. And so its name changed . . . Serendip, Ratnapida . . . Taprobane, Zeloan, Zeilan, Seyllan, Ceilon, and Ceylon — the wife of many marriages, courted by invaders who stepped ashore and claimed everything with the power of their sword or bible or language.

Ondaatje's family had been on the island since 1600, when the first known ancestor had arrived and, Ondaatje continues, "cured the residing governor's daughter with a strange herb and was rewarded with land, a foreign wife, and a new name which was a Dutch spelling of his own. Ondaatje." Since then, the Ondaatjes have prospered as doctors, preachers, lawyers, botanists, and tea-plantation owners. Some, especially Michael Ondaatje's paternal grandfather, Philip "Bampa" Ondaatje, took advantage of their knowledge of local customs, language, and law to establish their own fortunes. When the English imperialists discovered Ceylon, they became determined to buy up large tracts of land on which to build tea estates. The records of the Dutch and those kept by the villages themselves, when there were any, were often "inadequate," and men such as "Bampa," Christopher Ondaatje writes in *The Man-Eater of Punanai*, exploiting this inadequacy, "sometimes . . . abted for [their] own account, accumulating badly titled property and selling it cleaned up."

Even if Michael Ondaatje, on the day of his birth, could have seen the rich, red soil of the nearby Kuttapitiya Tea Plantation, with its thousands of tea bushes and its hundred workers harvesting the last of the season's pekoe leaves, he wouldn't have known that his father owned the land. Indeed, by the time Ondaatje was born, his father had mortgaged and sold most of the land acquired by his ancestors. The plenty and privilege and prosperity of the Ondaatje family in Ceylon were near an end.

FIGURE 2

What we think of married life: Doris and Mervyn Ondaatje.

By the time he was born, the tea estate was owned by Carson, Cumberbatch and Company Limited; Ondaatje's father, no longer its owner, had become one of its managers.

Even before Michael was born, his parents' marriage was near collapse, and, Kim Ondaatje explains, "by 1945, when he was two years old, his mother and father were divorced." After his parents separated, Ondaatje saw little of his father. After he reached adulthood, he never saw his father again. Until he was eight years old, visits were restricted to short vacations and special holidays. In the main, he learned about his father through stories. The closest link Michael had with Mervyn Ondaatje was by mail: he was encouraged to read the letters his father sent.

Michael often wrote back. In a way, he's never stopped writing to — and for — his father. A father was, in his mind, a figure that he could imaginatively piece together from different points of view: his mother's, his brother's, his sisters', and that construed from Mervyn's occasional letters. In all, it was a view based on a series of fragmented insights, often devoid of a full context or background. It isn't surprising, therefore, that in works such as *Billy the Kid, Coming through Slaughter*, and *The English Patient*, the "truth" of the protagonist's life has to be pieced together from whatever is available — a newspaper clipping, an anecdote, a bit of gossip, a hazy memory, a vaguely worded letter.

Although Ondaatje actively avoids voicing any explanations of the effect upon him of being separated from his father, *Running in the Family* suggests how much he needed to find him, in one form or another. As his older brother, Christopher, so succinctly put it: "In many ways my brother Michael's book is a love letter to the father he never knew, a large and glamorous man away in the distance." Kim Ondaatje adds, "In his youth, Michael missed out on the 'male' — the male role model his father might have provided." In *Running in the Family*, Ondaatje's view, from a distance, of his father's antics is a fascinating mixture of fiction and wish fulfilment. Philip Mervyn Ondaatje, when young, was charismatic, handsome, and charming, but as he aged, Ondaatje writes, he became a drunk prone to violent depressions and

13

dipsomania: "He couldn't eat, had to have a bottle on him at all times. If his new wife Maureen had hidden a bottle, he would bring out his rifle and threaten to kill her."

At times, the man could be gentle. He would take Christopher, his eldest son, on walks across the Kegalle tea estate, explaining the difference between orange pekoe, broken pekoe, and standard pekoe. "Mervyn Ondaatje was happiest doing the simplest things," explains Christopher: "being with his family, running the estate, discussing the books he was reading, teaching his children, talking to people. Somehow he thought he had to aim higher in order to be happy. He didn't have to. He shouldn't have tried to." Mervyn Ondaatje, simply put, was not a business man. He was, though, according to Christopher, a "snob" who refused to let his children consort with the servants or their children. Christopher remembers receiving a "hard slap" from his father after being caught at the servants' quarters: "The impact of his signet ring left a bruise on my cheek that lasted for days." Mervyn Ondaatje became, increasingly, the insensitive, self-absorbed drunk. Slipping further and further into alcoholism, he squandered what remained of the inherited family fortune, bungled his attempts to fulfil his responsibilities as a manager of estates for Carson, Cumberbatch, and, finally, failed to keep his marriage together. Things continued to get worse, and during the last year of his life (1965), Mervyn Ondaatje was reduced to running a small chicken farm.

In 1989, Christopher, like Michael in 1978 and 1980, felt compelled to return to Ceylon to find out how and why his father had failed so miserably. As Christopher recalls, the family's closest and most trusted friend, Hamish Sproule, could suggest only one answer: "Your father was ruined by debt, and I have always wondered why. . . . After all, drinking doesn't cost that much. . . . So why did he have to borrow? My guess is that he borrowed heavily to send you to England and to pay for your school fees!" If Hamish Sproule was right, Mervyn Ondaatje sacrificed a considerable portion of his income so that his eldest son could be a success — whether he realized that his destruction of the family fortune would also motivate his second son, Michael, no one will ever know.

According to Christopher, Mervyn's wife, Enid Doris, was born a Gratiaen, a member of a solid, "very proper Dutch burgher family." But she was also, when Mervyn Ondaatje first met her, a tall and elegant dancer in the tradition of Isadora Duncan, famous for performing unrehearsed and spontaneous rhythmic movements to music. Doris had the beauty and grace that Mervyn, as the wealthy owner of a colonial tea plantation, wanted in a wife, but she, in the end, could neither tolerate nor curb her husband's drinking. Since Michael Ondaatje had been too young to understand what was going on, he had to recreate his mother's efforts to make her husband accept responsibility. He writes in *Running in the Family*:

> Whenever my father would lapse into one of his alcoholic states, she would send the three older children (I would be asleep — too young, and oblivious) into my father's room. . . . The three of them, well coached, would perform with tears streaming, "Daddy, don't drink, daddy, if you love us, don't drink," while my mother waited outside and listened.

If, in the early years, the Ondaatjes' marriage was characterized by immature, excessive, and unrestrained frivolity — which they could easily afford to indulge in until the money ran out in the early 1940s — the increasing burden of four children and the constantly mounting debts sobered Doris into the maturity and responsibility her husband tried to escape. While Michael serves up an intoxicatingly romantic vision of his father in *Running in the Family*, Christopher, in *The Man-Eater of Punanai*, offers a less spirited but equally sympathetic outline of his father's gradual decline:

> In his youth, it's true, he had a wild period, characterized by extravagant fun and drunken escapades. Much of it can be

put down to his age and to the age in which he was young. . . . Unfortunately, he never got over the habit of drink. For most of the time that I knew him he was completely sober, but occasionally he went on a binge. He would start drinking as soon as he got up, then fall asleep from ten-o'clock until three in the afternoon, do a little work until about six, then go back to sleep for the night. When he was drunk, no one could predict what he would do, and we all feared him. . . . These bouts got worse and more frequent. . . .

While Christopher, being older, had glimpses of the father who might have been while having to endure the father who was, Michael was deprived of both. Only through the recollections of his mother and siblings did he have a chance to be near his father. Michael had to try to imagine; Christopher had to try to forget — and to forgive. It isn't surprising that both, in recounting their lives and their family history, reveal a marked tendency to blend legend and tale with rumour and hope.

At times both stretch the facts, but Michael, particularly, exaggerates his father's escapades into such a vividly imagined reality that one wants to accept every word as the literal truth. Ironically, some of his most incredible tales give accurate portrayals of the emotions involved — though they are quite fanciful in their ordering of events. Possibly the most vivid illustration is Michael's re-creation (in *Running in the Family*) of his father's infamous drunken binge in the summer of 1943. We are told that while Mervyn Ondaatje was putting on his brown leather army holster with shoulder strap — he was an officer in the Ceylon Light Infantry — he suddenly needed a drink. He began with a glass of gin, reached for a second glass, and then for the entire forty-ounce bottle. By the time he arrived at the railway station, Mervyn Ondaatje realized that he had forgotten his mission. He was to bring a fellow officer with him. So he hijacked the Colombo-Trincomalee train at gunpoint, forcing the engineer to do his bidding. When he realized he had dishonoured his uniform, he dropped his army pistol, stripped off his military attire, and retreated into the Kadugannawa Tunnel, where he fell into a deep depression. His wife, Doris, coaxed him out.

Although considerably embroidered, the tale is based on fact, as Doris Ondaatje confirmed to Kim during a visit in 1965. It seems that Mervyn, when drunk, talked bombastically, and on one occasion did manage to stumble into a bar car on a train wielding a gun, thereby frightening fellow passengers. On several occasions, he was said to have collapsed into fits of despair. In any case, Doris confessed that her strenuous, exhausting, repeated efforts to bring her husband out of his suicidal, depressive moods finally ruined her ability to live with and respect him. He became a mere shell of the man she had married. She finally divorced him in 1945.

ENGLAND, MY ENGLAND

After separating from Mervyn, Doris Ondaatje moved to Colombo, the capital of Sri Lanka, to be near her brother, Noel Gratiaen. Her aim was to settle her affairs. In *Running in the Family* we are told that "She got a job at The Grand Oriental Hotel," in Colombo, and there trained as a "housekeeper-manager" while the children went to local schools. In 1949, she decided to start her life again in England. England was, for her, the logical choice for a variety of reasons, the most important being that she was, as Christopher bluntly characterized her, "more English than the English."

She had always taken great pride in making certain that her children displayed her preferences: English dress, manners, speech, and education. She taught them the importance of correct table manners, and expected them to wear white shirts, perfectly pressed Oxford blue shorts, and matching knee socks. She had no use for the local Ceylonese garb — long loose shirts over shorts and sandals — and despised American blue jeans.

A more practical reason for choosing England was that her

former husband's sisters, Stephy and Enid Ondaatje, lived in Dulwich, and they had offered to help her establish herself. Ceylon had shed itself of British-colonial rule in 1948, and the newly formed Sri Lankan government was utterly unprepared for the extreme economic, social, political, and religious dislocations that resulted. Initially, Doris Ondaatje hesitated over her decision; there were, after all, four children involved. Stephy and Enid's invitation was tempting, but a new life in England still seemed an impractical dream. However, in 1948 Sri Lankan currency was devalued due to the fact that the British Bank was no longer stabilizing it, and, as a result, the value of Doris Ondaatje's divorce settlement was instantly reduced. Whether she stayed in Ceylon or left, she had few resources. As Kim Ondaatje explains, "She was a proud woman. After the final divorce settlement, she would accept from Mervyn only financial support for the children," but she determined to begin an independent life — even if it meant (and it did) running a boardinghouse in Lancaster Gate, England.

Lack of money forced Doris Ondaatje to live in the basement apartment of her own boardinghouse with oldest daughter, Janet, then thirteen. She withdrew Christopher, then fifteen, from the private school he had been attending (Blundell's, in Tiverton) and made room for him in the attic. Her hard work and efficient management of the business eventually paid off, and she was offered the job of managing the Café Royale, owned by Charles Forte, an investor in restaurants and banqueting businesses. By the early 1960s, she had become successful enough to afford her own flat on King's Road, Chelsea, and to travel to Paris, the United States, and Canada.

Things were also difficult for her emotionally in 1949. Until she was reasonably well settled, she also had no choice but to leave Gillian and Michael behind in Ceylon. In fact, Gillian never did get to join her family in England, and still lives in Jaffna, Sri Lanka, though she visited her mother in England and her brothers in Canada. It was not until the late summer of 1952 that Doris had earned enough to bring her fourth child, Michael, to England.

Continually separated from his father, and for a relatively short period from his mother, Michael Ondaatje's life in Sri Lanka was probably harder on him emotionally than he is willing to admit. Economically, socially, and culturally, he did not suffer. Despite hard times, Kim remarks, "he did have his own Nanny — who is still alive today [in 1992]." Gillian was close to him, and Christopher usually came to Ceylon for the summer holidays. Michael, in *Running in the Family*, records his recollection of his brother "borrowing a pakispetti box, attaching wheels, and bumping down the steep slopes." The two would have "daily arguments over Monopoly, cricket or marital issues."

Michael's "separation from his father affected him with a tremendous sense of loss," says Kim. "Luckily, though, as a boy he was influenced by a caring father figure," an educated, sophisticated, and sensitive man, his Uncle Noel.

BECOMING A FATHER IS EASY, BEING ONE IS HARD

Noel Gratiaen began his career as a lawyer in Colombo; success and respect earned him the position of judge in the same city. At the peak of his career, he became the attorney general of Ceylon. "After his retirement," Kim relates, "he moved to England to join his sister, Doris; and at times he lectured on law in American universities like Harvard. Probably his most bitter moment was when he discovered that the Ceylonese government refused to pay him the full pension he deserved."

For those who remember *Running in the Family*, Noel Gratiaen is the son of Michael's maternal grandmother, Lalla, who is carried off in the great Nuwara Eliya flood as if it were her "last perfect journey." Tales of Lalla's eccentricity, unconventionality, and irresponsibility are not simple exaggerations, for she did wander off, she did squat and pee in the local school yard, and she did gamble ferociously. Despite all the glorification of her idiosyncratic behaviour in *Running in the Family*, however, the brutal truth is, Christopher tells us, that she died in her sleep of alcohol poisoning.

Michael's portrait of the Gratiaens as one part hard work and two parts Rocklands gin is more fiction than fact. Not everyone in the family was so married to drink. Noel was solid and thorough, and he was probably as sensitive to the harsh facts of his sister's marriage to an alcoholic Ondaatje as Michael would later come to be. Still, there was one key difference: Michael would be granted the writer's ability to transform grief into personal, if fictional, consolation.

In any case, Michael Ondaatje prized two things: reading and education. As a boy, Michael seems to have had access to a considerable collection of books. But the only specific reference to any text of the period in *Running in the Family* is to the Kumarodaya first-grade reader. The flowing, cursive lettering that Michael Ondaatje still uses was formed by means of the exercises in this book.

Whether it was the result of Noel's decisions, or simply the family's way of doing things, Michael's education was as similar as possible to that of his siblings. Michael was sent to St. Thomas's College Boys' School, in Colombo, which Christopher had attended. In its "layout and architecture," the school "is undoubtedly a carbon copy of the English boarding schools of the Oxford/Cambridge model," wrote Darrol Bryant, who visited it in 1994 while on a trip to Colombo. "It's an impressive place, two blocks from the beach, with a large stone chapel, a main teaching administration building, and a residence encircling the huge enclosed field — called a 'cricket pitch' (I think that's what they call the playing area here)." It isn't surprising, therefore, that the school, before Sri Lanka's independence, had a curriculum designed to prepare students for an education in the English tradition, if not, eventually, in an English school. Even after independence, writes C.R. De Silva, "education [in Sri Lanka] retained a strong academic bias. . . . Literary courses were less expensive . . . and the British grammar school tradition lent greater prestige to academic studies."

By the fifties, when Michael entered St. Thomas's College Boys' School, postliberation changes to education had been instituted. Based on Education Act Number 5 of 1951, these changes only confused the system; they failed to improve it. The original languages of the island were introduced as an essential part of the curriculum, but there was also a new emphasis on Western science and technology, subjects for which these languages had little, if any, vocabulary. The result for many may have been, continues De Silva, a "warping of the whole curriculum." Michael expresses (in *Running in the Family*) the irony of what a beautiful but largely impractical language can do; he particularly emphasizes the grace of the Sinhalese alphabet, though all he remembers of it was that he used it to write such things as "We [rebellious, socialistic public-school children] must not urinate again on Father Barnabus' tires." The new education act was largely ineffectual; teaching, learning, and so on, were still predominantly based on a British model, and students were prepared for Cambridge, not for Ceylon. The emphasis was on the arts and British notions of culture.

Family and education, then, fostered the British streak in Michael Ondaatje — he still retains traces of a British-colonial accent. For those who remained on the island — or those without a literary bent — education in independent Sri Lanka may have been too literary, academic, British — in a word, inadequate. However, it was obviously an education that would benefit Ondaatje, for it put him in touch with the English literary tradition, one that he would later help to modify. This type of education, based as it was on British-colonial custom, culture, and language, contributed considerably to the character of the Ondaatjes' life in Ceylon: theirs was a "foreign" — a British-colonial — existence. The privilege of wealth and class, even though greatly eroded by the time he was born, made of Michael Ondaatje, as it did of many other members of his family, a stranger in a strange land, even the one he called home.

Possibly the main break from the British emphasis in this way of life came in the form of the newly imported American pop culture that affected the world so powerfully after World War II. Uncle Noel took Michael to see Gene Autry and Roy Rogers films, allowed him to play popular music on an old HMV record player, and tolerated, it seems, his passion for American comic books, especially those in the series entitled *Frontier News*, which glamorized the lore of the Wild West (see Freedman). "By the age of 8, the germ of the Western was in me," Ondaatje admitted to the *Globe and Mail*'s Pearl Sheffy Gefen, "and I dragged myself to see every movie made about Billy [the Kid]." Ondaatje's formal training was in British school English, but he found his im'ginative relief in American pop culture: "I grew up with this mythology of movies and comic books that came all the way from America to this tropical island."

BOARDING SCHOOL RITUALS

By July 1952, Doris Ondaatje was well enough established in her boardinghouse that she was able to have Michael brought to England. The two were briefly reunited in London, where they celebrated by going to the film *Wedding in Paris*. Then Michael was "whisked away," as Urjo Kareda tells us, "to the rituals of English boarding schools." He attended Dulwich College, in Mark Abley's words "a school for the genteel boys of upper-crust England," the alma mater of P.G. Wodehouse, Raymond Chandler, and Graham Swift. The Ceylonese and Sri Lankan education systems had been, to quote Swarna Jayaweera, "intended to meet the needs of children from well-to-do families. Their curriculum was modeled on that of prototypes [such as Dulwich College] in England. Their goal was to ensure success at the examinations of Cambridge and London Universities." Ondaatje's prep school had done its job well.

He had no difficulty adjusting to one system after the other. He had, in fact, been preparing for the move for a long time, because it would have occurred even if his parents had not separated and his mother had not moved to England. In an interview with Catherine Bush, he explained that he was fully aware of the British preferences of his family: "I was part of that colonial tradition, of sending your kids off to school in England. . . ." Although the Ondaatje ancestry is a blend of Dutch, Sinhalese, and Tamil (ancestors include illustrious members of the island's clergy and judiciary who can be traced back to the seventeenth century), much of the family was solidly British colonial in outlook. Dress, conduct, and education had to be, and largely were, English, which partially explains why Michael, even when he makes fun of the Cambridge-educated branch of the family, implies that although they ignored academics and frittered away a fortune, they could — no matter how drunk — at least correctly slur the King's English.

Ceylon, then, gave birth to Ondaatje, but England groomed him. He realizes that the shift offered him a different view of things, one that would give him a special opportunity. He told Linda Hutcheon that although he "grew up in Sri Lanka and lived in England for about eight years, and then came [to Canada]. . . . I don't feel much of 'England' in me. I *do* feel I have been allowed the migrant's double perspective, in the way, say, someone like Gertrude Stein was 're-focused' by Paris." Once in England, he became obsessed with reading; he confessed to Bush that he "was a compulsive reader all through my teens." "I think I did write one short story," he said to interviewer Jon Pearce, "but I didn't have much interest in writing at the time. I had read a lot, but had actually no interest in writing."

Although he has positive memories of learning about literature, he has stronger recollections of his negative experience of English schooling, especially his downfall in math. In all, he got on well with other students and participated actively in rugger and swimming. Although his report cards are unavailable, his overall work appears to have been more than satisfactory, for he was allowed to enter the B.A. program at Bishop's University in Lennoxville, Quebec, immediately upon arrival in Canada. Even if he prefers to play down his academic skills by maintaining that he was more absorbed by the songs of the Coasters than concerned about his competence in math, Michael Ondaatje was, in fact, quite a solid student.

FRIENDLY SIBLING RIVALRY

In 1962, when Ondaatje was nineteen, an age, he told Hutcheon, "when everyone changes, when everyone wants to remake themselves," he chose to come to Canada. As he stresses, he was "lucky to come then and go to university then." But his choice wasn't merely accidental. Who knows where he might have gone had Christopher not made a crucial decision himself. Christopher Ondaatje realized that England provided few opportunities, and that a return to Sri Lanka would mean entering a world of social and political upheaval and conflict. He had made, therefore, what he called his first "business decision": he chose to immigrate to Canada because it offered the best hope. After the family fortune had been lost, Christopher went to work in London at the National Bank of India. He was seventeen years old at the time, and "no longer a rich boy with the world at my feet." Although Christopher's ambitions were modest at first — for he had had to begin as a trainee — he candidly admits that, since he already had British tastes, he soon "acquired British ambitions as well as British methods." Initially he planned to work for the bank for a while and then return to Ceylon, but in the meantime he was offered a position in Canada. There he would discover what his brother, Michael, would soon realize: "I had been forced to become independent, and now independence seemed strangely invigorating. I was determined to make my own decisions without depending on anyone else."

Christopher began his career in Montreal, as a banker, and was reasonably well established by 1962. He then encouraged his younger brother to join him. Although today known mainly for his business acumen — in financing, investments, and publishing — Christopher also had literary ambitions. In fact, he would go on to write various books: two volumes on the prime ministers of Canada, *Olympic Victory* (Christopher was a member of Canada's Olympic bobsled team when it won a gold medal in 1964), *Leopard in the Afternoon, The Man-Eater of Punanai*, and even a novel under a pen name. Literary ambition had struck him first, but the tide turned. Don Gillmor quotes his terse explanation: "I started in the literary world and got caught up in the madness of the business world." The two brothers, then, had more in common than just family and some shared experiences: each had an interest in literature and sought a place where he could make his mark. Christopher led the way to Canada, and Michael followed.

The family's version of the story is that the brothers met in Montreal, where Christopher was working for the investment firm of Burns Brothers. Michael then headed off to Bishop's University in Lennoxville, convinced by his brother of two things: first, that in Canada success was dependent upon a reasonable level of higher education, and second, that Bishop's University, with its Church of England affiliations (the Ondaatje family, for several generations, had belonged to the Church of England), was the right place to go. Though Christopher had headed off to write books and found himself deflected into the world of high finance, he would never fully abandon his literary ambitions, and so began what Michael would one day call "a friendly sibling rivalry" (see Gefen).

THE TRUE VALUE OF A TEACHER

Bishop's College, the forerunner of Bishop's University, was founded in Lennoxville in 1843 by George Mountain, the Anglican Bishop of Quebec. Attending Bishop's was undoubtedly significant for Michael Ondaatje because there he met numerous people who would, in later years, directly and indirectly shape his life. One such individual was Ralph Gustafson. Gustafson was a Bishop's graduate and, by the time Ondaatje arrived on campus, he was a professor of English as well as poet in residence.

FIGURE 3

Arthur Motyer teaches.

He would read and comment on some of Ondaatje's earliest poems.

Ondaatje also met George Whalley at Bishop's, just outside McGreer Hall, the oldest building on the campus. At the time a professor at Queen's University in Kingston, Ontario, George Whalley (according to Elizabeth Whalley) "was a committed high Anglican, and he kept his connections to Bishop's and often lectured there or set up poetry readings." This short meeting would be the start of a long, close relationship between Whalley and Ondaatje. Whalley casually mentioned that he had invited the British poet W.H. Auden to read at Queen's, and Auden had accepted. The reading took place on 8 March 1963, and Ondaatje, at Whalley's invitation, was in attendance.

A knowledge of Auden is one of the keys to understanding Ondaatje's early poetic technique, most importantly his handling of irony. Ondaatje, however, had this to say in a 1984 interview with Sam Solecki: "Everybody talks about Auden's influence on me but I've never read much of his work." In the same interview, he can only meekly admit that the line "no instruments / agreed on a specific weather" (from the poem "Dates") is his "most conscious borrowing from anyone." The line is based on similar phrasing in Auden's "In Memory of W.B. Yeats," a poem Ondaatje heard — although he prefers not to mention that — at the Queen's reading. Ondaatje didn't have to read much of Auden; Auden read his work to Ondaatje.

The most important thing to occur on the Bishop's campus for Ondaatje and lovers of Canadian literature, however, happened in a classroom. Professor Arthur Motyer taught two courses in literature during Ondaatje's first year as an undergraduate: the first was English 319: Modern Poetry — American and Canadian, and the second was English 316: Victorian Literature. Motyer inspired in Ondaatje, then just nineteen years old, a love of literature. He required his students to read *Modern Poetry*, edited by Mack, Dean, and Frost, and E.J. Pratt's *Ten Selected Poems*. Motyer had a particular passion for Browning's dramatic monologues, such as "My Last Duchess," and he read to his students from *Victorian Poetry and Poetics*, edited by Houghton and Stange, with such passion that he immediately made the young and impressionable Ondaatje want, as Gefen reports, to "be Robert Browning, so [he] started writing monologues."

It was the teaching style Motyer employed, above all, that made the difference. Ondaatje credits Motyer (in an interview published in *Manna*, for which he provided written responses to questions posed by an anonymous interviewer) for introducing poetry in "the best possible way." Here's how Ondaatje described the experience to Solecki in a 1975 interview:

> [Motyer] also taught drama and he read beautifully. He'd come into class and read a Browning poem and the poem became an acted thing, a passionate thing. He aroused an enthusiasm for literature. I think in teaching it's not so important that a student learn anything specific but that an enthusiasm be communicated; and Motyer had that real love of literature.

Motyer's approach linked directly to what Ondaatje felt, and still feels today, was crucial to any literary experience. Ondaatje told Bush:

> For me, the greatest pleasure of literature is reading as opposed to writing. I write as a reader. I don't want to write something that wouldn't interest me as a reader. For me, the process of writing, therefore, has to be a learning or discovering as opposed to just a telling or an entertaining. Reading is that great intimate act, between reader and author, reader and book. It's sacred to me, that relationship, and involves trust, surprise, and is ideally a continuing relationship.

Motyer did more than enflame Ondaatje's feelings for poetry: he taught him the power of stage drama. He adapted Herman Melville's short story "Billy Budd" into a verse play called *Innocence at Sea*, and he encouraged Ondaatje to take the lead role. Ondaatje was unsure and insecure; he hesitated to take on such

FIGURE 4

Michael Ondaatje as Billy Budd in Innocence at Sea.

an important role. His first close friend in Canada, Ken Livingstone, who had already established his reputation as an actor at Bishop's (and who would in later years direct Ondaatje's first effort to present *The Man with Seven Toes* as a verse play), convinced him to accept Motyer's offer. Although Bishop's University did not yet have a proper theatre (the Bishop's University Centennial Theatre officially opened on 8 July 1972, ten years later) Ondaatje accepted. With minimal props and lighting, the actors carried the play off successfully on a makeshift stage. Ondaatje, as an unnamed reviewer noted, "fit into the lead role of Billy Budd beautifully, with all the innocence and modesty shining through" (see "Speaking Play").

Up until that night, Ondaatje had only participated in one or two plays, and his initial hesitancy was partly based on his rather humiliating debut. Michael, according to the eyewitness account of Kim Ondaatje, had had only a few lines in one scene of his first play (the name of which Kim can't remember), but his performance was unforgettable: "Michael was so memorable because the moment he stepped on the stage, he forgot the two or three lines he had. After being prompted, he managed to utter his phrases mechanically and exit."

Once he had won success as Billy Budd, Ondaatje was able to laugh with his friends about the earlier episode, but not everything could be laughed away. Six months after arriving at Bishop's, he realized his financial resources were running out. Christopher, who had supported his younger brother for the first year, was broke. He had lost the first fortune he had made ("like many a financier, he's made and lost a few fortunes in his time," says Kim).

To help Ondaatje out of his immediate straits, one of his English professors, Doug Jones, invited him to move into his home, which he shared with his wife and their children. Recognizing that Ondaatje was an immensely talented student, Jones encouraged him to apply for grants, fellowships, and scholarships. But even if Ondaatje was granted funds, there would be a waiting period. Until something better came along, Ondaatje was encouraged to stay with the Joneses as a guest. During his first year of studies, Ondaatje won the President's Prize for English (1962), but no money came with the award. Tuition fees were only two hundred dollars, but residence fees were four hundred dollars per term, cash Ondaatje didn't have, so he accepted the Joneses' offer, and joined the family in their North Hatley home on Houghton Street.

A POET'S GUEST

Doug Jones taught at Bishop's from 1961 to 1963, after which he joined the faculty of the University of Sherbrooke. Before going to Lennoxville, Jones had published his first collection of poems, *Frost on the Sun* (1957). The year before Ondaatje arrived, Jones had completed his second volume, *The Sun Is Axeman* (1961), for which he won the Governor General's Award. Jones was a generous and responsive teacher who often invited students to his home for dinner. Young student writers stayed late into the night, and they were encouraged to read and discuss their poetry.

Jones recognized Ondaatje's talent immediately, and he conscientiously helped to guide the young writer to an understanding of writing techniques. Perhaps not because of this direct guidance, but certainly because of the direct encouragement, Ondaatje began to write poetry seriously. More importantly, Jones turned Ondaatje's attention to specific Canadian writers and their images and metaphors, to the ideas Doug Jones would later outline in his book *Butterfly on Rock* (1970). For the young poet there was now a sense of a new tradition being formed, a new, vigorous, and vital outlook on the world, one that linked to, but significantly differed from, the British tradition in which he had been educated in Sri Lanka and England. Jones offered him a sense of freedom and possibility. Ondaatje, along with the major British and American poets he admired — such as Auden, Yeats, Eliot, and Pound — now began to read the Canadians Jones was introducing to him.

FIGURE 5

Doug Jones at Bishop's University.

Summers were spent at the Joneses' cottage, Keewaydin ("home of the wind"), near Bancroft, Ontario. The place was described by A.J.M. Smith in "Keewaydin Poetry Technique" and by Michael Ondaatje in "Eventually the Poem for Keewaydin." Because Doug and Kim Jones were both university teachers (Kim lectured at the nearby University of Sherbrooke), Ondaatje, at Keewaydin, was introduced to numerous prominent figures in the Canadian literary scene, especially those linked to McGill University, such as Louis Dudek and A.J.M. Smith. They came to relax, and only after swimming and boating and sunbathing did they retreat to a secluded spot near the shore to work on their poetry. Ondaatje, still only nineteen years old, found these encounters with well-known writers a little overwhelming. In his poem about Keewaydin, which was published in *The Dainty Monsters*, he described the period as "Two years of coming here / and seeing others write poems. . . ."

THE STOLEN BRIDE?

Kim Jones, an intelligent, beautiful, graceful, artistic woman, was to leave her husband for Michael Ondaatje. Was Ondaatje the guilty Paris who stole Helen from another man? Ondaatje's poem sequence "Troy Town" (in *The Dainty Monsters*) deals with Homer's tale of the kidnapping of Helen by Paris, and at least two critics, Susan Glickman and Nell Waldman, have suspected that Ondaatje was indirectly writing about himself and Kim Jones. Kim, however, assures me that the stuff of her relationship with Ondaatje belongs to prosaic documentary, not to poetic epic.

Kim's version of how and why she left Doug Jones is far from romantic, and holds no mythological parallels. She explains that her relationship with Doug had deteriorated long before Michael arrived at Bishop's. The breakup was more than imminent; it had already taken place, although she and Doug kept it to themselves. Doug and the children stayed in North Hatley, and Kim kept a place in Lennoxville, closer to her part-time job as a lecturer at the University of Sherbrooke. Without fanfare, they lived much of their lives independently and discreetly; their four children would be affected by anything they chose to do. The fact that Kim and Doug were teachers with public positions and reputations also prompted their discretion.

Kim remembers quite clearly that her first meeting with Ondaatje lacked any tinge of romance, and was far from scandal provoking. One evening Doug brought a few bottles of wine and several promising young poets to Kim's place in Lennoxville to hold a poetry workshop. The instant Kim heard Ondaatje's work, she says, she "knew he was a poet." She immediately noted that the reader of the poem she had just heard had an extraordinarily handsome face, tousled hair, unavoidable pale-blue eyes, and an attitude that made him seem not aloof but somehow apart, separate. She did fall in love with him instantly, but she did not give in to her emotions right away — he was, after all, her husband's student.

The relationship developed gradually. Doug and Kim Jones knew that their marriage was at an end. There was "no deception, no betrayal," says Kim, and, above all, no stolen bride. By the time Kim had become involved with Michael, she and Doug were long past being husband and wife in any sense except the legal one; they were good friends, and they wanted to stay that way.

KIM CLOSE UP

Kim Ondaatje was born in 1928, in Toronto, and was baptized Betty Jane Kimbark. Her mother was a Harris, a member of the family that owned the enormously successful Massey-Harris company. Kim was, like Michael Ondaatje, born into a family of wealth. Although she had incurred her mother's wrath by marrying a poet, her family eventually tolerated her marriage to Doug Jones.

FIGURE 6

Kim Ondaatje.

Her father was Frank Marston Kimbark, an industrialist who owned, among other things, a printing business; he had given his daughter a sense of the value of art and a love for the visual. He prized his fine collection of nineteenth-century etchings, engravings, and paintings, which he kept on the walls of the family home, placing one on top of the other. When viewing the collection, one would have to lift etching after etching, as if each grouping were a calendar.

Like Michael, Kim is a confident and passionate individual. Unlike him, she is outspoken and quick to correct mistaken views about her life or her opinions. She proudly discusses her remarkable family lineage, which can be traced back to Lord Culpepper, who, she claims, lost his head for love because he was caught in bed with one of Henry VIII's wives. She had repudiated the wealth and social connections her family had to offer, while Michael had had those advantages withdrawn from him due to the actions of his drunken father. Kim severed her ties to her family because she decided to marry a promising poet, Doug Jones, refusing to hold out for the socially correct mate her family might have preferred.

Unlike the shy, nineteen-year-old Michael Ondaatje, Kim Jones — then thirty-four — had already established herself. She was a teacher, a painter, a photographer, and a filmmaker, and her work had received considerable attention from reviewers. She had attended Havergal College, Toronto, and, following her graduation, had completed one year at the Ontario College of Art before transferring, in 1949, to the Department of Fine Arts at McGill University in Montreal. She had an artistic temperament and flair, and must have reminded Ondaatje of his own mother, Doris, and maternal grandmother, Lalla. While studying at McGill, Kim acted as independently as the women of the Gratiaen line described in *Running in the Family*. Kim was expelled from art classes after a conflict with her teacher. Throughout her life she has had her own fierce standards, and she has always resisted being pigeonholed. David Pulver has quoted her as saying, "I'm a multi-media artist. . . . I've used graphics, paintings, film and still photography to express my ideas. . . . I don't fit into any category. I cross the lines between art and film." In our personal interview, she underscored her stubborn independence by insisting that she "was absolutely misquoted by the reporter [Pulver]." Yet, the description seems so apt that, even if she didn't say it, she probably should have.

In any case, the expulsion from classes did not affect her career; she simply completed a B.A. in honours English instead. She graduated in 1952, and won prizes and fellowships to Queen's University for several achievements, including short-story writing. While working on her B.A. at McGill, she edited the student literary magazine called *The Forge* and a young-writers' issue of the prestigious *Northern Review*. At Queen's University, she received her M.A. in English in 1954, and proceeded to teach literature for the next five years at various places, among them Waterloo Lutheran (now Wilfrid Laurier University) and the University of Sherbrooke. Her training in literature, and her strong artistic sense, made her one of the most important and influential readers of Michael Ondaatje's work, especially in the early years of his career. In fact, in his handwritten dedication to Kim in his first published book, *The Dainty Monsters*, Ondaatje says that the collection was "begun in Lennoxville in 1962 [where he had first met Kim], and was finished [while he was living with her] in Kingston in 1967, and shown to her in its various stages."

A MEXICAN DIVORCE

In 1963, less than a year after Michael had been invited to live with the Joneses in North Hatley, Kim and Michael began living together in Lennoxville. They maintained this arrangement for several months. For Michael, the notion of having children out of wedlock was intolerable. He wanted, in Kim's words, "all his children to be Ondaatjes." Quebec law would not recognize divorce, even of non-Catholics; only Mexican law allowed for quick, easy separations. To be certain there would be no legal snarls or delays, Doug Jones accompanied Michael and Kim to Mexico, where, Kim says, he "signed the necessary papers." There was no ill will among the three. After the legal matters were cleared up, the couple got married in Concord, New Hampshire, because that state recognized a Mexican divorce after a three-day residence. This requirement was especially easy to fulfil because part of Kim's family lived in New Hampshire. The ceremony took place in Concord's Congregational Church on 12 June 1964. Michael was twenty-one; Kim was thirty-five; and their first child (Quintin) was to be born in twenty-five days (on 7 July 1964).

Doug Jones had dealt with the situation graciously, but, since comments about his wife's marrying one of his students might be both difficult and embarrassing for him, as well as for their own four children, it was decided that the newlyweds would move out of the Lennoxville community. They left for Toronto, where Michael continued to study for his B.A. at University College, University of Toronto. The couple continued their friendship with Doug Jones, and when Michael and Kim's first child was born, Doug was asked to be the godfather, a role he gladly accepted.

TORONTO LIFE

City life offered Kim and Michael the possibility of privacy. Yet, for Michael, marriage was a rather sudden responsibility. Kim, of course, had experienced marriage and was the mother of four. Michael, the young married student, could only note, rather humorously (in the notes-on-the-authors section of Raymond Souster's anthology *New Wave Canada*), that "children keep arriving," though in fact they had only two, Quintin and Griffin (born in 1967). A situation that might have become insurmountably problematic was eased by family help. Brothers on both sides assisted the couple. Kim's brother helped by offering the couple a place to live — the third floor of a house on Hawthorne

Street, facing Osler Park. Michael would put Quintin in a stroller and take her to the park, while Kim studied the shades and textures of the park's bushes and trees, searching for new subjects to paint.

Christopher Ondaatje, now quickly gaining a reputation as a major financier on Toronto's Bay Street, lent a hand by getting Michael a summer job as, in Kim's words, "a medical aid in a mental hospital near Mimico, run by a Dr. Temelcoff, a name he would borrow later for a character in *In the Skin of a Lion.*" Michael had no medical training, so his main duties were general clean-up work. It was in this institution that he gathered his first direct impressions of the madness, insanity, and silence that would later dominate his book *Coming through Slaughter.*

While being provided with a place to live by his brother-in-law and a job by his own brother, Ondaatje first heard about the odd conjunction of the Taylor brothers. One brother, E.P. Taylor, was a well-known businessman and racehorse owner; the other, Frederick B. Taylor, was a socialist who gained a reputation as an artist; his painting *Hull Riveting* was used on the front cover of the McClelland and Stewart edition of Ondaatje's *In the Skin of a Lion.* Sometimes the accidents of history seem as meaningful as the events of a novel.

A year later, in 1965, the Ondaatjes moved to Sussex Avenue, near the soon-to-be-built Robarts Library in downtown Toronto. Michael realized that, given the demands of a wife and child, he would have to establish his credibility as a poet if he was going to make writing his career. He remembers paying increased attention to the advice he received from editors. He explained to Jon Pearce that

. . . Milton Wilson of the *Canadian Forum* . . . took great trouble with the poems. Not only did he take some poems for the *Forum*, but he wrote back and made comments about them. Once he gave me good advice which I didn't take. In "Pigeons, Sussex Avenue," he thought there were a couple of lines that were unnecessary; but I was convinced they were crucial and the poem was published in the magazine as it was. Later, when I was editing *The Dainty Monsters*, I realized he was quite right and I dropped the two lines — about three years too late.

Ondaatje became more and more exacting about his own work. In fact, in later revisions, *more* than two lines were dropped from "Pigeons, Sussex Avenue." The seventeen-line poem was trimmed to twelve lines by the time he finalized the manuscript of *The Dainty Monsters*. He would rarely leave a poem alone if he felt it had a flaw. Throughout his career, this kind of determination has revealed itself. In the first anthology Ondaatje edited, *The Broken Ark: A Book of Beasts* (1971), for example, he cancelled the last line of his own contribution, the poem "Birds for Janet: The Heron," just as the book was being printed. (The line was "time to go to school.") A narrow strip of paper was pasted over the extraneous line on the pages of the final versions of all the books that were already bound. Then the book was packed for delivery to bookstores. Kim remembers that the final manuscript of *In the Skin of the Lion* was considerably larger than the printed novel. Ondaatje recalled his most recent work, *The English Patient*, at the last moment. He revised its ending, he explained to Vicky Gabereau in a radio interview, and then allowed it to be released. The desire to get things right has remained strong in Ondaatje throughout his career.

O CANADA, OUR HOME
AND NATIVE LAND

If Ondaatje had reservations about remaining in Canada, they were dispelled when he made a return trip to England in March 1965. He, Kim, and Quintin, then eight months old, paid Doris Ondaatje a short visit. The trip confirmed for him his alienation from the country and its culture. On his return he became a Canadian citizen. The ceremony involved was actually a rather unpleasant experience for Ondaatje; he was asked to swear allegiance in a rather depressing, dilapidated building. He jokes that while answering the standard questions posed to all immigrants he couldn't get one answer right, but was accepted nevertheless. To Urjo Kareda, who was writing an article on him for *Saturday Night*, Ondaatje overdramatized his naturalization, and, perhaps, misrepresented the true nature of the journey to England that preceded it. He almost suggested that both were part of a rite of passage that he had to undergo if he was to commit himself to the nation he now fully accepted as his homeland, an act that he had to perform in order to prepare himself psychologically to rough out his first book, *The Dainty Monsters*. Stan Dragland, Ondaatje's close friend, assures me that Ondaatje's rather theatrical account of his acquisition of citizenship is more fiction than fact — though Ondaatje, so far, hasn't cleared up the details. Dragland, Tom Marshall, and Stuart MacKinnon, three writers who knew Ondaatje very well, are always prepared to emphasize the difference between Ondaatje the man and Ondaatje the image, and they rightly warn anyone who cares to listen that Ondaatje can spin a lovely tale, or a sad tale, and not just in his writings.

It seems likely that Michael and Kim Ondaatje's primary reason for travelling to England was to be with Doris because she had just received news of Mervyn Ondaatje's sudden death. In a drunken stupor he had fallen forward and cracked his skull open on some cement patio stones. The news came as a terrible shock. Ondaatje's poem "Letters and Other Worlds" (published in *Rat Jelly*) comes to terms with his father's life as a "terrifying comedy" of alcohol and outrageous acts. It "was probably the most difficult poem for me to write," said Ondaatje in a 1975 interview with Solecki; "it was about 4 or 5 times as long as it is in the finished version. I cut it down so that it would be suggestive as well as descriptive, suggestive of things that aren't or can't be said." Mervyn's death, then, sent Ondaatje to England, but, by speaking to Kareda about "alienation" and "naturalization," he managed to avoid revealing his private pain in *Saturday Night*. For

FIGURE 7

*Michael Ondaatje as a graduate of
the University of Toronto, 1965.*

Ondaatje, poetry was the medium in which to grapple with personal distress.

Ondaatje did, finally, become a Canadian citizen, and, after the trip to England, put considerable effort into finalizing his first book. But of central importance to him that year was his need to come to terms with the death of a father he had known mainly through letters from Sri Lanka, a place that seemed to the new Canadian quite another world.

FIRST AWARDS AND THE COACH HOUSE CONNECTION

While he earned his general English B.A. at the University of Toronto, Ondaatje gradually gained notice for his poetic talent. He won the Ralph Gustafson Award in 1965; a year later, he received the Norma Epstein Award for Poetry. The two prizes confirmed for Raymond Souster that Ondaatje's work was worth including in a new collection he was putting together. Entitled *New Wave Canada*, it was to become a central anthology of the time. In 1966 Ondaatje tied with Wayne Clifford for the E.J. Pratt Gold Medal for Poetry, which was also awarded by the University of Toronto. Clifford remembers that the committee from University College wasn't

prepared for a tie. There was only one medal, and only one cash award of five hundred dollars. Michael wanted the money — as a young married student he needed it. He was awarded the medal. I wanted the medal, but got the cash. The irony of it all was that although we both won, neither of us got what we really wanted.

This odd conjunction of victory and failure cemented their friendship. Clifford was linked to the relatively new, but increasingly important, publishing house called Coach House, then located off Bathurst Street, and took Ondaatje there to meet everyone involved. The Coach House connection would last many years, although no one then realized that Ondaatje was to become one of the press's editors. At Coach House, Ondaatje was introduced to people who would quickly change the direction of his career. Gradually, Ondaatje came to know not only authors such as bpNichol, Roy Kiyooka, Bob Fones, Frank Davey, and Victor Coleman, but also the founder and printer of the press, Stan Bevington. "I don't know why," says Wayne Clifford,

> but the moment Ondaatje and Bevington met, they got along like a house on fire. Both especially admired bpNichol's notion that an artist should have control over his own book. Nichol had the ideas, but Bevington and Ondaatje had the imagination to understand Nichol's ideas, and to act on them.

Since bpNichol, Wayne Clifford, and Stan Bevington emphasized direct contact with the manuscript, Ondaatje began to envision preparing all the elements of his own book: the presentation of the poems on the page, the design, the cover. The sense of a book as an entire aesthetic experience fascinated Ondaatje. His link to the press would, over time, both liberate and discipline him.

CHOOSING A PATH AND A GUIDE

In the summer of 1965 the Ondaatjes went north to a rented cottage near Bancroft, Ontario. There Michael met David Secter, a director and filmmaker who offered him the job of special assistant for his movie *The Offering*. Ondaatje was also given a bit part in the film — he played a reporter. By his own account, he fared well when helping behind the scenes, but not in front of the camera. Speaking of his performance to Solecki (in 1975) he declared, "You mustn't mention this. . . . That was the worst scene in the film." But the passion to direct was born in Ondaatje during the making of *The Offering*. Indeed, he has always hoped to gain recognition as a serious film director, a goal that has so far eluded him. No matter how serious his ambitions were at the time, though, the plain fact was that the young, recently married new father, with only a B.A. in hand, simply lacked the financial resources necessary for the risky venture of independent film-making, and so he turned his mind back to his education.

He did have some reservations, however. As Kim puts it, "There's always a danger for the creative mind in advanced study. Graduate schools can kill creativity." But since Ondaatje had won an Ontario graduate scholarship for the upcoming academic year, the question became not so much one of whether to go, but where to go. As Kim had had a bad experience as the result of making the wrong choices at McGill, she was eager to help Michael select both the right graduate program and the appropriate thesis supervisor.

They narrowed the field to two possibilities: Northrop Frye at the University of Toronto and George Whalley at Queen's. Kim had known both men for a considerable time, and to her they exemplified the extremes that academia could offer. Frye, from her point of view, "was clearly too systematic, too abstract," as demonstrated by his theoretical works *Fearful Symmetry* and *Anatomy of Criticism*. George Whalley, though equally theoretical, placed emphasis on the process of writing rather than on the product, as suggested by the title of his book *Poetic Process*. Furthermore, Whalley had written and published poetry, something Frye had not done, so Whalley could be expected to comprehend the schism between creativity and scholarship that Ondaatje was experiencing. Kim feared that the academic system might turn Michael's attention from "the development of his own artistry to the analysis of the artistry of others." They discussed the matter for several weeks. Ondaatje remembered meeting Whalley at Bishop's a few years earlier and accepting his invitation to come to Queen's for W.H. Auden's reading. He recalled getting along with Whalley very well. Kim pointed out that Whalley and his wife, Elizabeth, had acted almost as spiritual counsellors for her while she was in the process of leaving Doug Jones. Finally, Kim says, she and Michael agreed that Whalley was the best choice for Michael.

So Michael, Kim, and Quintin made the move from Toronto to Kingston, where Michael began his graduate work. From September 1965 to September 1967 he worked to complete his M.A. courses and his thesis, "Mythology in the Poetry of Edwin Muir: A Study of the Making and the Using of Mythology in Edwin Muir's Poetry" (1967). The topic reflects Ondaatje's obsession with myths, especially with how a few sparse facts can suddenly become an entire intricate history. In the *Manna* interview, he elaborated:

> I am interested in myth. Making it, remaking it, exploding [it]. I don't like poems or works that cash in on a cliché of history or a personality. . . . Myths are only of value to me when they are realistic as well as having other qualities of myth. Another thing that interests me about myth is how and when figures get caught in myths.

Ondaatje's thesis carefully traces how Muir used personal experience and linked it to larger myths of universal value. The melding of the private and the universal fascinated Ondaatje. He organized his thesis argument to isolate three possible means of connecting everyday human experience to larger, universal patterns. His divisions were based on the immediate and private, the mythic, and the historic. For him, these three levels formed a template with which to gauge the universal. Interestingly enough, Ondaatje didn't merely study the three levels; he internalized them and then used them as the blueprint for grouping the poems in his first book, *The Dainty Monsters*. First come local poems about love and children; the "Troy Town" poems, based in mythology, follow; and this section includes, towards its conclusion, two historical poems about Elizabeth I. Like Muir, Ondaatje, as he stated in his thesis abstract, wanted to "harness . . . 'images' with 'words.' "

The thesis demonstrates that Ondaatje was deeply concerned with the problem of whether great art is local, or universal, or both. His interest in mythos, archetypes, and universals offers us insight into the shape of his early imagination. His intellectual discipline compelled him to write exacting, tight poems, which he then strictly ordered in *The Dainty Monsters*. Even a cursory reading of the thesis reveals a great deal about Ondaatje's own art, as well as Muir's. Here's how he put it in his abstract: "I discuss the poems where Muir *made* myths: out of his own life, his insights into Eden and the Fall, and his visions and dreams." The study, in effect, represents Ondaatje's urge to give shape to the local and the particular while, at the same time, linking the immediate to the cosmic. It is an analysis obsessed with how things are ordered.

A FAILURE TO RESPECT PROSE

George Whalley — a poet, a critic, a teacher, an Oxford scholar, and, above all, a Canadian often mistaken for an Englishman — was undoubtedly the right choice for Ondaatje's thesis supervisor. He helped Ondaatje to shape his thesis into its final form, while being a sympathetic reader of the young poet's first poems. Irving Layton, with his usual zest for iconoclasm, ridiculed (rather unfairly) Whalley's impeccable accent, which "makes even Englishmen / wince, and feel / unspeakably colonial." Layton's irreverence reminds us that Ondaatje's English education in Sri Lanka and England, would — and did — suit Whalley's approach and manner. The two got on extremely well. Whalley was committed to the tradition of valuing education for its own sake, and his graduate teaching relied on establishing a kind of student-tutor relationship. He guided Ondaatje towards self-development and personal vision rather than just a degree. A Ph.D., in itself, had no value to Whalley, who admired scholarship for its intrinsic rewards. Ondaatje more than accepted this view — he shared it. He never enrolled in a doctoral program, and even now refuses to obtain that degree simply for form's sake.

FIGURE 8

George Whalley and parrot.

Whalley influenced Ondaatje in profound ways. Ondaatje has confessed that Whalley one day said to him, "You don't respect prose as much as you respect poetry, do you?" Ondaatje's later tribute to George Whalley's memory, from which this question is quoted, shows that if the young author ever did lack respect for prose, he has certainly made up for it since (see "Michael Ondaatje"). Ondaatje praises Whalley in this written remembrance, which is based on a beautiful interplay of language sensitive to everyday ironies and incongruities. Ondaatje recalls that Whalley's favourite pet had been a parrot. Is it, Ondaatje wonders as he praises Whalley's skills, mere coincidence that the mindless parrot, which only echoes what it hears, should be the favourite pet of an intellectual who could never get himself to parrot anything, who was so "Un-parrot-like"? Fearing that some might find the notion of parroting denigrating, Ondaatje wrote, in a letter to Michael Moore, the editor of *George Whalley: Remembrances*, "[I]f Liz [Whalley] wants anything cut (ie parrot?) that will be fine." The section was left in. Elizabeth Whalley told me that she recognized "Michael is like that. . . . And George would have understood."

THE DAINTY MONSTERS

While living on William Street in Kingston, Ondaatje began to explore the shapes *The Dainty Monsters* might take. The task was difficult for him. Because he wanted to develop his impressions of the Kingston-Gananoque-Bellrock region of Ontario, many of the poems were revised to mute some of their initial exotic or Ceylonese qualities, although Ondaatje obviously didn't want to erase all traces. Of the influence of Ceylon on his work, especially at this point in his career when he wanted to be considered and accepted as a Canadian poet of importance, he could only allow (in the *Manna* interview), "It is there I suppose, but not in any conscious way. There are a couple of poems which refer to images of Ceylon, but mostly I was concerned with coming to terms with the present landscape of that time." From the poem "Over the Garden Wall" he cut an extended passage that included exotic animals, such as elephants and camels, never to be found in the "present landscape" of Kingston and its environs, a landscape to which he tried to give shape. He wanted to be accepted as a Canadian, he didn't want to seem foreign or different, and during a radio broadcast (entitled "The Charm of Kingston") he made a point of the fact that the material he wrote about centred on Kingston's landscape, "where the sense of history lives for me."

The Dainty Monsters in its final form reveals numerous important influences: Arthur Motyer's emphasis on the dramatic monologue; George Whalley's sense of a poem as part of the unified structure of the book that contains it; and, finally, Wayne Clifford's belief in the need for each poem to be able to stand on its own. Ondaatje's blending of these views shows his admiration for the poet as maker. As he explained to Jon Pearce:

> The thing here is to remember constantly that the poem is not real life; the poem is a poem, the poem is a work of art. It's an artifice, it's a chair, it was made by somebody, and what is involved is what happens when you put the chair into a room. What is involved also is how the person made the chair, and what is important is the other chairs the person has made.

The aesthetics of the well-made poem and, most importantly, the ability of the poem to be separated from its author, were crucial concerns of the young poet as a naturalized Canadian. His intellectual training reinforced the notion that art was, somehow, at its best when it was impersonal. Yet his instincts as a writer were different: as the numerous poems he has written about friends, family, marriage, and love reveal, much of Ondaatje's richest, most vivid art borders on the confessional or takes the form, on some level, of memoir. The division between training and instincts is an issue that Ondaatje does not wish to explore. He demands, and his attitude seems almost paranoid, that people read his book or poem rather than his life, even such a poem as "Kim, at Half an Inch" (which he included in *Rat Jelly*). It focuses on his own wife, in his own bed, "half an inch" away:

> hooked so close
> her left eye
> is only a golden blur
> her ear a vast
> musical instrument of flesh

The notion of a poem as a chair seems rather stilted in this context; the confessional and the impersonal make, sometimes, odd bedfellows in Ondaatje's work and in his explanations of his artistry.

Ondaatje, then, is clearly articulating the aesthetic ideals of the modernist tradition, though in his writing he only partially practises them. He remembers being nurtured on the moderns. He read them with care. His M.A. thesis is filled with quotations from the works of Ezra Pound, William Faulkner, George Orwell, Wallace Stevens, and W.B. Yeats — the dominant influences of the time. His relatively new Canadian influences, such as D.G. Jones, A.M. Klein, Phyllis Webb, Margaret Atwood, and Raymond Souster, were largely under the sway of modernism as well, and their stances as poets, at the time, often simply supported the notions that dominated the British literary tradition.

The tension it embodies between impersonal art and personal life — and the instant when an experience is truly made into a poem — is probably what makes Ondaatje's work so captivating, so honest. Even when a poem is concerned with technique, the true lived experience it records is never annihilated or overlooked. As he expressed in the remarks he published with his poem "Peter" in a 1970 anthology, he sees what is happening in a poem as if it were "a home-movie. I am still conscious of all the bits and pieces / relatives and friends that were just to the left of the camera and that never got into the picture." The lively life he shared with family and friends provided much of the subject matter of *The Dainty Monsters*, but, again endeavouring to keep the balance between art and biography, he maintains that he "can't remember what was off-screen when writing [the poem] 'Peter.' " For many readers, the notion that art is only for art's sake makes it seem cold and artificial, and so Ondaatje also tries to personalize his work: "Peter," he suggests, "probably contains my most interesting hang-ups." He even adds, rather enigmatically, that his "appendix burst a few days after I finished the poem."

After completing the final editing of *The Dainty Monsters*, he set to work preparing it for Coach House (selecting his paper, typeface, cover, and so on). While Michael was thus occupied, Kim, though pregnant with Griffin, born later that year, was also putting in time at the press, working on a series of her own lithographs. Kareda relates Stan Bevington's recollection of how determined Ondaatje was to finish the book in time for it to be considered for the 1967 Governor General's Award. This first book, dedicated to Kim, so carefully edited and prepared, limited to three hundred fine copies, did not win.

FIRST STEPS TO A CAREER

Ondaatje graduated from Queen's University in 1967 with a Master of Arts degree, and was offered a one-year teaching contract at the University of Western Ontario. The position wouldn't begin until September 1968, but a Canada Council Grant helped defray some expenses and provided support during the final stage of trimming his manuscript of *The Man with Seven Toes*.

With great expectations, the Ondaatjes arrived in London, Ontario, where they rented a place big enough to house their own children as well as Kim's four children from her first marriage, "although rarely," Kim says, "did all six stay in the house at the same time." Their domain was on Piccadilly Street (mentioned in Ondaatje's poem "Postcard from Piccadilly Street" in *Rat Jelly*, and used as the setting for Kim's Piccadilly Series paintings). Kim continued painting and sold her work as quickly as possible to help support the family, but these sales did not bring in a great deal of money. Michael, Kim claims, had asked her not to teach at Western so that there wouldn't be competition between them, and he had also asked her not to do interviews with various magazines — he thought that it would disrupt their family life. He felt most comfortable when she kept her personal and family life as private as he kept his.

Clearly, in some ways, Michael was affected by Kim's lack of a job, but he encouraged her to paint. They did need financial help, though, and it was provided, Tony Urquhart told me, by Kim's mother,

> an extremely wealthy woman [who] kept the brakes on things. She helped them live in comfort, but she wouldn't support anything lavish. It was more than gossip only a few months after the Ondaatjes had moved to London that Kim&s mother was disappointed that her daughter had run off... but that's her story. ... The end result is that Michael Ondaatje was able to concentrate on his teaching, while Kim stayed home to paint.

Ondaatje taught at the University of Western Ontario from September 1967 to April 1971 while completing the final version of his long poem *The Man with Seven Toes* (1969); a critical study entitled *Leonard Cohen* (1970); his Governor General's Award-winning *The Collected Works of Billy the Kid* (1970); *Sons of Captain Poetry* (1970), a film about the concrete poet bpNichol; and, finally, an anthology of animal poems, *The Broken Ark: A Book of Beasts* (1971). Despite his new teaching load, this period was certainly the most productive of his early career.

It was not until 1969, two years after the publication of his first book, *The Dainty Monsters*, that Ondaatje felt completely comfortable with the influences of other writers and new techniques. His apprenticeship stage was at an end. *The Dainty Monsters* was the offspring of the British-Canadian tradition, presided over by the modernists Auden and Yeats, but *The Man with Seven Toes* was a work quite different in nature and technique. Arthur Motyer, Ondaatje's inspiration at Bishop's, had encouraged him to look at the possibilities of blending dramatic verse and the Browning monologue, especially in terms of its links to the modernist tradition as manifested in such writers as T.S. Eliot. Ondaatje had already modified this technique in the "Troy Town" poems of *The Dainty Monsters*. Later, at Queen's, George Whalley had encouraged Ondaatje to study carefully Edwin Muir's method of linking private experience, history, and mythology. Ondaatje's first effort to bring the two together in the elevated mythical and historical material of Homer's Troy now seemed an overly studied use of history. It was the work of a young man eager to put his university education to use, and there was a facile element in the way he transformed family events into poetic experience. Ann Mandel writes, "As Ondaatje recalls it, his friend the poet David McFadden told him 'no more Greek stuff.'"

THE MAKING OF *THE MAN* ## *WITH SEVEN TOES*

In *The Man with Seven Toes*, Ondaatje achieved his first sustained poetic voice. It let him speak, he admitted to Catherine Bush, without feeling self-conscious: "there was a jump from the self to a mask of some kind." In part the long poem allowed for theatricality, but it also allowed for an exploration of the single voice bordering on madness. With *The Man with Seven Toes*, Ondaatje was able to construct a story line by drawing on research, a method that would increasingly influence his way of writing.

He had actually begun working on the poem as early as the fall of 1966. He'd spent the summer working as a flagman for a

City of Toronto road-repair crew (it was, Ann Mandel quotes him as saying, "the nearest thing to desert I could get"). On the job, he witnessed the accidental death of a fellow worker. Shaken by the experience, he recorded it in a moving poem called "For John, Falling," published in *The Dainty Monsters*:

> a doctor, the foreman scuffing a mound,
> men removing helmets,
> the machine above him
> shielding out the sun
> while he drowned
> in the beautiful dark orgasm of his mouth.

By the time *The Dainty Monsters* was published in 1967, he had completed the first draft of *The Man with Seven Toes*. Ken Livingstone, a friend since Bishop's University days, so liked the draft that he, with Ondaatje's collaboration, worked it into a dramatic stage production for three voices to be presented at a Vancouver theatre festival in 1968. The Vancouver production was reasonably successful, so another effort to present the poem as drama was made by Paul Thompson, of Toronto's Theatre Passe Muraille, at the Stratford Workshop in 1969. Despite the efforts made to transform the poem into a viable drama — with Ann Anglin, Paul Thompson's wife, drawing on all her skill to breathe life into the role of the main character, Mrs. Fraser — the results, Ondaatje admitted to the *Globe and Mail*'s Herbert Whittaker, were all too obvious: "it lasted 20 minutes. It didn't really work that well."

The stage productions, however, certainly helped Ondaatje visualize how a dramatic poem flowed as a unit. The final form of the poem, he realized, had to be altered and tightened. It was at this point that the most significant influences on the final written structure were exerted. One came from Phyllis Webb, especially her book *Naked Poems*. Ondaatje, in an article called "Roy Kiyooka," has called *Naked Poems* "one of the most beautiful and influential books for any young poet today." In his 1975 interview with Solecki, he credits Webb with showing him how to keep a long poem unified:

> she talks about a narrative form as a kind of necklace in which each bead-poem while being related to the others on the string was, nevertheless, self-sufficient, independent, lyrical. That got me really interested in the form for *The Man with Seven Toes*.

The other influence was from Ondaatje's close friend Stuart MacKinnon. Ondaatje had been reading and making comments on MacKinnon's manuscript version of *The Intervals* (1970), a book that he admired (as he went on to tell Solecki) because, like the poetry of Edwin Muir, "it starts from the personal and moves out." MacKinnon thus, by example, reinforced for Ondaatje the direction his poem should take.

Ondaatje seems to have been engaging in his close reading of Webb's and MacKinnon's poetry about the time his interest in a particular Australian artist was piqued. In the same interview he told Solecki,

> There's a series of paintings by Sidney Nolan on this story [which served as the basis for *The Man with Seven Toes*] and I was previously interested in Nolan's Ned Kelly series. I got fascinated by the story of which I only knew the account in the paintings and the quote from Colin MacInnes. That's how it grew.

That may have been how the poem grew, but Ondaatje's interest in the story on which it is based and in Nolan's art began much earlier, when he was a student at the University of Toronto in 1965. At the Toronto Public Library, he and Kim saw a special exhibition dedicated to Nolan's paintings and the Australian folklore and legends that inspired them. Ondaatje began to explore the artist's past; Kim remembers going to the library for him to dig up some of the books that related to the topic. That

FIGURE 9

Sidney Nolan (Australia, 1917–1992), Death of Sergeant Kennedy at Stringybark Creek, 1946, enamel on composition board, 91.5 x 122.0 cm. Gift of Sunday Reed, 1977, collection of the National Gallery of Australia, Canberra.

Nolan's work was of more than passing interest is confirmed by Michael and Kim's acquisition of one of his paintings: *Constable in the Marsh.* Kim recalls that after they sold the painting, years later, the new owner began to find it so dark and brooding and depressing that he soon put it back up for auction.

Such a brooding quality appears to have been typical of Ondaatje's preferences at the time; he seems to have been obsessed with works that stressed the dark and the violent, the harsh and the brutal. Nolan's Ned Kelly Series utterly absorbed him. Nolan, to get a sense of Ned Kelly, an outlaw (Kim named him "the Robin Hood of Australia") whose actions resembled those of the American Billy the Kid, pieced together a portrait by reading books, newspaper clippings, and the *Australian Royal Commission Report* of 1881, and by listening to recorded ballads. Nolan's technique of coming to terms with this bushranger — idolized by some and despised by others — suggested to Ondaatje a way of creating his own picture of Billy the Kid.

Ondaatje's immediate concern, however, was a second series of paintings by Sidney Nolan: a sequence of portrayals in oil of the adventures of an escaped convict named Bracefell and a Scottish lady, Mrs. Eliza Fraser, shipwrecked off the Queensland coast. Ondaatje purchased a book entitled *Sidney Nolan* (edited by Kenneth Clark, Colin MacInnes, and Bryan Robertson, first published in 1961), and studied its plates. They offered an overview of Nolan's career as a painter. (The book is still in Kim's personal library.) As Ondaatje started writing *The Man with Seven Toes*, he realized he had no sense of the Australian landscape, and so had to rely on the descriptions offered by Alan Moorehead's writings. In the 1975 Solecki interview he concedes:

All the geographical references in the book are probably wrong and I'm sure all Australians think that the book is geographically ridiculous. . . . I was putting geographical names into the latter cos I liked the sound of them. Chupadero Mesa, Punta de la Glorieta. The sound of words was something that concrete poetry woke me up to at that time.

By 1970, Ondaatje's reputation was well established, and he was often invited to read at universities. One memorable reading took place during a poetry festival held at Bishop's in 1970. Ondaatje read with his friend bpNichol. Nichol's concrete and sound poetry didn't go over well. He was accused of not being a "real" poet. Soon the debate turned to the issue of what constitutes a Canadian poet. Ondaatje remained silent, even uninterested. In fact, one commentator (Elizabeth Rodriguez, who reported on the festival for *Fiddlehead*) claimed that Ondaatje seemed to find the topic "pointless." When he finally spoke, he rejected any narrow definition of the Canadian poet, and endeavoured to keep the focus away from either nationalities or individual experiences. He restated his belief that readers should pay attention to the poem, not the poet. Since then, he has also maintained that many writers divert attention from their work by drawing attention to themselves. To Jon Pearce he remarked:

> I'm often horrified when I hear a poet talking on about a poem he's written. Often this happens at readings; people over-expand before they've read or over-expand after they've read or in a question period go on about the poem or what they wanted to do. For them to have to do this, the poem has failed in some way. I would rather try it over again when it's failed, but I think it's the duty of the poet to remain silent.

It was possible for him to simply "remain silent" about his own poetry, but, as a critic tackling Leonard Cohen's writings in a study for McClelland and Stewart's Canadian Writers Series he had to come to terms with his views on two related issues — a writer's life and a writer's work. As might be expected of a man who wishes to be left alone himself, Ondaatje courteously skimmed Cohen's biography and compressed it into a few insubstantial pages, for "nothing," he declared in *Leonard Cohen*, "is more irritating than to have your work translated by your life." As soon as he could, he dismissed the issue of the writer's life by emphasizing that Cohen had "cleverly incorporated the prostitution of personality that comes with success."

He concentrated instead on assessing Cohen's achievement as a writer, and explored the complexities of Cohen's narrative technique. Yet, no matter how objective he tried to be, Ondaatje's most penetrating insights into Cohen were almost always indirect self-revelations. His focus on Cohen's use of American pop-culture figures, for example, reflects his own interest in such characters as Billy the Kid and Pat Garrett. For Ondaatje these figures represent the destructive force of American imperialism.

Although short, and at times idiosyncratic, Ondaatje's assessment of Cohen's work is unquestionably insightful commentary, as well as an indirect rationale for Ondaatje's next venture: *The Collected Works of Billy the Kid*, an experiment with point of view.

Ondaatje had written the draft of the study of Cohen during the summer of 1969; he proofed the galleys in 1970 while staying at a rented cottage near Gananoque, Ontario. He had received a small research grant from the University of Western Ontario in the summer of 1969, and so was able to make a quick trip to the Jewish Public Library in Montreal to prepare a preliminary bibliography. He then went to Toronto to listen to CBC Radio tapes of Cohen interviews, supplied to him by Cohen's editors at McClelland and Stewart. Finally, he borrowed a sixty-minute tape of a Cohen interview from his friend and future colleague at York University, Eli Mandel, and went off to the cottage for the summer.

It was a tremendously important summer for Ondaatje. He has never denied that Cohen's novel *Beautiful Losers* was the most important influence on him as a young writer in the process of moving from poetry to prose. In his Cohen study he wrote that it was "the most vivid, fascinating, and brave modern novel I have read." Its effects on Ondaatje would reveal themselves explicitly in *The Collected Works of Billy the Kid*.

THE KINGSTON CONNECTIONS:
A FLASHBACK

While supervising Ondaatje's thesis at Queen's, George Whalley had extended his student's social circle. He had invited Michael and Kim to the numerous parties for graduate students the Whalleys held at their home. Ondaatje met several memorable people on these occasions — particularly Stan Dragland, who was to become his closest friend. The two hit it off immediately, and for more than thirty years they have been doing something or other together, whether it be simply taking walks, writing poems for each other, or discussing life while canoeing from one Algonquin Park campsite to another. It was Dragland, in fact, who introduced Ondaatje to canoeing, and since then, Kim claims, Ondaatje has become one of the activity's most ardent fans. Ondaatje describes his friendship with Dragland as "Stan and I laughing joking going summer crazy" in a wonderful poem entitled "Walking to Bellrock" (published in *There's a Trick with a Knife I'm Learning to Do*). The spontaneous Ondaatje, rarely seen, is probably most familiar to his "crazy summer friend," Stan. The two have similar temperaments and similar senses of humour. Both delight in practical jokes. Kim remembers how, on one occasion a few years after the two first met, Michael and Stan spent an afternoon "dressing up my favourite cow, Beulah, in rubber boots and straw hat so that they could take photographs" of the animal to liven up a slide show dealing with family events.

For Ondaatje, the Whalley parties in Kingston could not have happened at a better time. The mid- to late sixties was probably the most intense, ambitious, and active period of the Kingston literary community, which included a group of poets — among them Tom Marshall, David Helwig, Gail Fox, and Stuart Mac-Kinnon — that would later be called the Kingston Poets. Ondaatje's involvement with this group, and the literary community that contained it, was indirectly facilitated by an earlier collaboration. As a Bishop's undergraduate he had edited a small

FIGURE 10

Michael Ondaatje, cover drawing for The Mitre.

magazine called *The Mitre*. Excited at being granted his first opportunity to contribute to a magazine, he had produced a cover drawing for the publication. Here, in the oldest student journal in Canada (it was founded in 1883), Ondaatje published his early work (some of this work, such as "Scenes, After a Line by Thomas Carlyle" and "In Search of Happiness," has never been republished). He showed his *Mitre* efforts to George Whalley, and, because he was committed to bringing writers and editors together, Whalley introduced Ondaatje to some local figures. In fact, Kim remembers, Ondaatje met two especially important and enthusiastic young writer-editors, Tom Marshall and Tom Eadie, at one of Whalley's Garden Island Cottage parties. This meeting, in turn, sparked new friendships and new opportunities for Ondaatje.

Eadie and Marshall had transformed *Quarry* from an annual student publication into a distinguished quarterly. They co-edited their magazine with the assistance of several equally aggressive and ambitious young guest editors, including David Helwig and Douglas Barbour. As a student at the University of Toronto, Ondaatje had published two poems in this rising little mag, and two years after his arrival in Kingston, he, too, became one of *Quarry*'s guest editors. Ondaatje told Pearce that "there was a lot of conversation about writing among us," and Marshall remembers that they sometimes exchanged poems: "Everyone exchanged poems. Mike Ondaatje, the visiting D.G. Jones and I read new poems at one another at Mike's place in the city on at least one occasion." Ondaatje took over editorial duties when Marshall went off to do further graduate work in England. He prepared a special cover for one 1967 issue (it featured zebras because, by this time, his animal poems had become one of his trademarks). Kim worked at his side, and her name is listed in several issues as the person in charge of subscriptions.

After Ondaatje had begun to teach at the University of Western Ontario in 1967, he continued to support *Quarry*. When no less a writer than Mordecai Richler went out of his way to snub *Quarry*, dismissing it as "parochial," Ondaatje jumped to its defence. Of course the magazine is parochial, he argued in an article called "Little Magazines/Small Presses 1969": that "is precisely what most little magazines are proud of being. They are a private, local, regional art form." His own editing of a special edition of *Quarry* two years earlier, however, seemed to adhere more closely to the editorial policies of the *Tamarack Review*. In the same article, Ondaatje called this magazine's commitment to publishing "the best writing in Canada" "the height of presumption," but his disdain must be tempered by a careful look at his practice. He did include in *Quarry* writers who were local and regional, such as David Helwig and Stuart MacKinnon, but he also selected national voices, such as Margaret Atwood, Claude Bissell, Ralph Gustafson, Doug Jones, Gwen MacEwen, and John Newlove. He did not hesitate to offer a strong selection of the best, a selection that would help establish him as a credible editor. Ondaatje's rather rapid rise from contributor to guest coeditor and editor of a special issue was partly attributable to the fact that the Kingston literary scene at that time was in high gear and such opportunities were available (to the right person) for the taking; but Ondaatje's rise was, surely, also the result of his own ambition and determination.

THE LEFT-HANDED CANADIAN COWBOY

Shortly before completing *The Man with Seven Toes* and the draft of *Leonard Cohen*, Ondaatje reached a point when he felt ready to tackle the material he had accumulated on Billy the Kid. He began by reflecting on the ideas he had derived from Sidney Nolan's Ned Kelly Series. Nothing seemed to click. He picked up Edmund Wilson's *Patriotic Gore* (1962), Ann Mandel tells us, "with the vague intention of writing a Civil War story or poem." But his instincts said "Go west, young man." He turned to the few poems he had written using the voice of Billy the Kid, and suddenly the legend of Billy merged with his memories of playing cowboys and Indians as a child in Ceylon. After that there was no hesitation; he wrote *The Collected Works of Billy the Kid: Left Handed Poems* over a period of two years, and took another year to edit and rearrange the manuscript. Whittaker quotes Ondaatje as saying that he was never "interested in the real Billy the Kid. In fact, I think he was probably a dull, boorish character." The Billy in his poem, he told Bush, is very different. He is an alter ego:

> *Billy* is a personal book, very much about my world then, even though it's set in a different country and it's about an absolute stranger to me. I found I could both reveal and discover myself more through being given a costume. I could be more honest about the things I wanted to talk about or witness.

The way he chose to deal with his alter ego in writing was, at first, so private that only Kim and his friends knew he was working on something new. As he was nearing the completion of the first draft, Kim suddenly guessed that the subject was Billy the Kid, probably because Michael was taking photographs of their son, Griffin, sporting a cowboy hat and plastic pistol. He would not admit that she was right. When he had finished, he asked her to be the first to respond to the manuscript. He handed it to her, he told Solecki in 1975, and

> went for a very long walk while she read it. I had no idea at that point what it was like, whether it was good or whether it was garbage. That's why I don't like talking about what I'm writing right now. I don't want to be influenced during the actual writing by anyone. I want to climb all the possible branches.

In the signed edition of *Billy the Kid* that he gave to Kim, Michael wrote that he had been living "in Billy's head," and then, quoting the French composer Erik Satie, he confessed: "I am having a poor time dying of sorrow; everything I timidly undertake fails with a boldness never before known."

He had few preconceptions about Billy when he undertook the project. He began to search for a link between mythology, history, and biography, a quest that recalled his study of Edwin Muir. Billy the Kid seemed an ideal subject, for Ondaatje had long harboured an interest in him, and was bothered by the way he had been mythologized. "I was sick of the clichés," he told Bush, "the hip versions of him that reduced the danger of such a figure. I wasn't interested in appropriating him as a mythic figure, it was much more a personal enquiry."

Ondaatje won the Governor General's Award for *Billy the Kid* in 1970. The judges were amazed by its daring experimental techniques and its brilliant recreation of the American West of Billy (William Bonney) and his pursuer, Sheriff Pat Garrett. Although Ondaatje denies that he was looking for a new form, it is clear that with this book he had shifted to the experimental aesthetics typical of Coach House publications: he had created a collage of photographs, lyrics, ballads, short prose narratives, interviews, and found poems. This looser structure allowed him to construct his own myth about the young killer and his nemesis. By now, having edited and reviewed a number of Coach House books — with their odd shapes and sizes, their blending of prints, photographs, and text — Ondaatje had the knowledge he needed to explore the full range of the technology the press offered.

If Ondaatje was delighted to have control over the shape and design of the book, he was discontented with Coach House's limited distribution network. This was such a serious issue for him that he reached an important decision. ("He had to make a choice at some time," remarks Kim.) He chose to have the book printed and designed at Coach House, thereby fulfilling his aesthetic interests, and published and distributed by House of Anansi in Canada and Norton in the United States. The combination of good design and good distribution, he felt, would allow his book the greatest chance of success.

The photographs that crop up throughout *Billy the Kid* make the book extremely appealing because they lend it an air of historical authenticity. In fact, some of the "historical" pictures were actually taken by Ondaatje himself. There is, of course, at the end of the book, the well-known portrait of Ondaatje, as a young boy in Ceylon, dressed in a cowboy outfit; but other photos, too, were manufactured for the book, such as the one of Stuart and Sally MacKinnon, posing as western settlers, seated on a porch.

Ondaatje had always been interested in the camera — in fact it was an obsession. Stuart MacKinnon claims that "one hardly ever saw him without one." "He had a good eye, a good sense of what would make a photograph. But he was especially good at catching people in revealing poses, or, more often, deliberately getting people to pose. He liked choreographed photography," Tony Urquhart told me. "In fact, I remember that on one occasion he asked me and my wife to pose in 1880s fashion, and then asked me to put on a kind of demented look while wielding an axe. He then took the shot."

The photographs and the physical appearance of *Billy the Kid* were only two elements of its form. Other elements — the ordering of sections, the diction, the tone — were another matter. Ondaatje often asked his friends to look at final versions of his manuscripts and to make suggestions as to what should be included or struck; he had done this with *Billy the Kid*. Anansi, however, had required Ondaatje to work diligently with a house editor — Dennis Lee — and this was a rather new and different experience for him. Lee acted as "midwife," and he aided Ondaatje in transforming a very private work into a very public one. In his article "The Case of the Midwife Lode," Mark Witten quotes Ondaatje commenting on why Lee's contribution mattered so much:

As an editor [Lee] gets completely involved with a work. It's not a professional commitment. It takes over his life. . . . As far as I could see, he was the only editor I could trust with the manuscript. As a critic, Dennis is pretty brutal. He doesn't like bullshit. At one point he wants you as a writer to clarify all the intricacies of your work. He tests you with ideas and if you [don't] argue back with him it can be deadly. You need someone as brutally honest as you would be with yourself — a kind of alter ego or devil's advocate. He made *Billy* more public in a way. It was a very introverted book. He helped me to take it and turn it into a universal rather than just a very personal thing.

Much of the editing was done by mail, partly because Ondaatje's hectic teaching schedule in London prevented him from driving to Toronto on a regular basis to discuss various revisions, but also because Ondaatje didn't feel totally comfortable with having to do what he had always tried to avoid: clarify what he thought he was doing as a writer. When asked about this, however, he directs our attention to a less plausible, though more humorous, rationale: "It's better to work with Dennis by mail because you don't have to deal with his cigars" (see Witten). Ondaatje chain-smoked Craven A menthol cigarettes at the time, so this explanation, of course, doesn't hold water; it's yet another diversion that allows Ondaatje to conceal his private views.

Dennis Lee also became the editor of Ondaatje's next book, *Coming through Slaughter*. Ondaatje's tribute to Lee is frank and honest, but he is reluctant to explain just how he clarified some parts of the manuscript that Lee insisted were simply too private, too personal. Ondaatje resists making either his correspondence with Lee or his revisions public. (Although he has sold many of his papers to the National Archives of Canada in Ottawa, the public does not have access to them.)

ONDAATJE BEATS THE DRUM

While the final galleys of *Billy the Kid* lay on the dining-room table of his home on Piccadilly Street, Ondaatje sat back and skimmed the *London Free Press* entertainment section. His eye was immediately drawn to a small article on Buddy Bolden, the jazz musician who went mad while marching in a parade. This simple newspaper commentary sparked the thought processes for what Ondaatje would call, according to Kim, his next "very personal book." Kim remembers the excitement Michael expressed at finding the column in the local paper, but she knew better than to ask specifically about the subject of his work, "for he always kept that to himself." Tony Urquhart, who, with some other friends, was spending the afternoon at Kim and Michael's, didn't realize how serious, if not absolutely superstitious, Michael was about not discussing his work in progress. Urquhart spoke about his own work, and then asked Ondaatje what he was doing. "Ondaatje, in a very serious, committed, confidential voice, told me," says Urquhart,

I'm working on an opera for three rats. The hard part is describing the feet; they're so tiny you know, so detailed. I believed him, of course . . . I mean, he sounded so sincere. It was the laughter behind me, of those who knew Michael better, that suddenly told me I'd been put on.

Once the joke was over and the guests had left, Ondaatje, as was his habit, made some initial notes, and then began to research his idea. Several years later, in 1973, he drove through Slaughter, Louisiana, to give himself a fuller sense of Buddy Bolden's world and experience. Kim accompanied him, and, she remembers, she drove "while Michael took and read notes. He knew exactly where he wanted to go, what he wanted to do and who he wanted to see."

What he kept to himself at the time, though, was a personal memory of having once, like Buddy Bolden, marched in a parade. While a student in England, at Dulwich College, Ondaatje had joined the school cadet corps and become a drummer in the corps band. He remembers wearing long striped pants and a jacket with gold regalia. In 1993 he told Vicky Gabereau about following at the rear of a corps parade one day, striding along, mechanically pounding a military march on his drum, daydreaming of just wandering off into a side street.

69

The germ of the novel about Buddy Bolden had, therefore, actually been planted in Ondaatje when he was still a teenager, but had taken firm root only in 1970. At that time, his immediate project was something quite different: a film about bpNichol entitled *Sons of Captain Poetry*. That Ondaatje should display such a high level of interest in the type of poetry his friend Nichol produced — sound and concrete poetry — may, initially, seem surprising. Ondaatje's own aesthetic was clearly conservative by comparison. Speaking to Solecki in 1975, he accounted for his interest in concrete poetry in this way:

I'd just finished the actual writing of *The Collected Works of Billy the Kid*, and there was a real sense of words meaning nothing to me anymore, and I was going around interpreting things into words. If I saw a tree I just found myself saying tree: translating everything into words or metaphors. It was a very dangerous thing for me mentally and I didn't want to carry on in that way. I just felt I had to go into another field, something totally visual.

Ondaatje had explored the form himself. His efforts include at least three short concrete poems: "Aardvark" (1969); an untitled work published in Nichol's magazine, called *grOnk* (here is the entire poem: "I've never read a line / of Gertrude Stein"); and, finally, "Silver Bullet" (probably written in 1970). This third poem, claims Nichol, is "a discarded version from his Billy the Kid series."

Ondaatje did create a fourth concrete poem. "Somewhere around this time [1970]," verifies Dragland, when Ondaatje "seems to have been working in various media, he pasted" together a "collage poem" of Billy the Kid. It appears to have been a parodic reworking of the photograph of the young Ondaatje in a cowboy suit included at the end of *Billy the Kid*. Ondaatje photocopied the photograph, enlarged it, and pasted words on it in such a way that they would appear, he commented in an interview with Douglas Barbour and Stephen Scobie, to go in "one ear and out the other." Even if Ondaatje is indulging in fabrication here, his words suggest how tired he'd become of *Billy* by the time he had written the final version.

CAPTAIN POETRY

To some degree, working with bpNichol offered Ondaatje emotional and psychological relief from his own introspection. More importantly, Nichol had become one of his closest friends, and Ondaatje was determined to make a film that would provide full insight into his poetry and poetics. Ondaatje applied for a Canada Council grant, and received $2,500 to make the film.

He had not worked on a film since 1965, when he had worked under David Secter during the making of *The Offering*, but he had absorbed numerous skills that helped him to master the techniques of directing. Although he had relatively little experience with the medium, he had had an undeniable passion for movies ever since he had first seen Roy Rogers on the screen. Since then, however, Ondaatje had studied more sophisticated examples of the art; Sergio Leone's *Once upon a Time in the West*, he told Solecki (in 1975), is "one of my favourite movies." Ondaatje knew the details of the movie so well that he was able to identify Leone's influences with ease: "[T]here's a scene [in *Once upon a Time in the West*] where just before the family is shot all the birds fly off which Leone has literally taken from John Ford's *The Searchers*; the shooting through the boot is from a Gene Autry film and so on." Ondaatje's film may not have had the budget of a popular Western, but his funding was sufficient for his purposes. He wanted to reveal bpNichol's special sense of poetic form. He was determined to avoid producing a film that resembled a slick CBC documentary. His aim was to offer a personal, intimate view of his subject, to create, in Kim's words, a "film on Nichol as he saw him. It's not just a film of his friend; it's an interpretation of him and his art."

Unstructured, exploratory, impulsive — the making of *Sons of Captain Poetry* was more a matter of patching footage together after the fact with the aid of cameraman Bob Fresco than of carefully planning and organizing a plot structure in advance. In an effort to be true to his subject, Ondaatje allowed impulse to be his guide, and he remembers driving with Fresco up and down Toronto's Yonge Street in search of variations of the letter *A* — small *a*, capital *A*, neon *a*, painted *a*, and so on. Nichol wanted to call the film "I Dreamed I Saw Hugo Ball," emphasizing the inspiration he had found in the dadaist movement, but Ondaatje had images of comic-book heroes and pop art firmly in mind. The dadaists, under the influence of Hugo Ball, a German actor and playwright (1886–1927), had delighted in the creative potential of chance and accident, of random, illogical juxtapositions. Ball and his friends often placed large canvasses on the floor and literally threw words and letters onto them, producing a collage effect. Nichol discussed his dadaist precursors in the film, and Ondaatje did try, to some degree, to incorporate their ideas into the filmmaking process.

After *Sons of Captain Poetry* had been completed, Ondaatje, speaking to Barbour and Scobie, referred to himself and Nichol as "Hollywoodish" and as "arch-romantics," ignoring the fact that most Hollywood films are meticulously planned, structured, scripted, and directed. Ondaatje wanted to stress that the unplanned had its own artistic dimension, its own order, but as the filming progressed, he began to let Nichol chat on and on, and often failed to pay sufficient attention to the sound quality; as a result the sound track is extremely muddy. Nichol, too, worn down by the demanding shooting schedule, resisted posing and scripting. Ondaatje told Barbour and Scobie that, at one point, impatient with Ondaatje's pace, Nichol "put 8 Beach Boy LPs on in a row! . . . [N]early gave me a breakdown." Ondaatje was forced to take extra editing time in an attempt to impose some semblance of order on the film.

All the clowning around involved in the making of the movie was great fun for Nichol, Ondaatje, and Fresco. Ondaatje explained to Barbour and Scobie that he had contributed to the spirit of the proceedings by declaring that his inspiration had been a dull, glib Hollywood movie, *The Joker Is Wild* starring Frank Sinatra. Despite the efforts of everyone involved, *Sons of Captain Poetry* never really achieved a coherent shape, and Ondaatje publicly shrugs it off by claiming that they celebrated the completion of their work by going to another B-grade Hollywood movie, *Beyond the Valley of the Dolls.* Privately, though, he felt tremendous disappointment that the film received so little recognition. He was especially unhappy that it was not shown at the Canadian Film Awards because, in the words of Ron Evans, film and literary officer at the Ontario Arts Council (interviewed by Robert Fulford on CBC Radio), it lacked a "proper category."

BEYOND THE LEFT MARGIN

Sons of Captain Poetry took two weeks to shoot and two months to edit. Despite the uproarious good times those involved shared in the course of its creation, Ondaatje still managed to learn one serious lesson from Nichol and three other sound poets — Steve McCaffery, Paul Dutton, and Rafael Barreto-Rivera — collectively called the Four Horsemen. With concrete and sound poetry, Ondaatje explained to Barbour and Scobie, "You're put in a world where there's nothing to catch hold of easily. Like writing poetry when you've escaped the comforts of the left-handed margin. . . ." That may be why Ondaatje used the subtitle *Left Handed Poems* for *The Collected Works of Billy the Kid.* Literally, of course, Billy the Kid was left-handed, but Ondaatje seems to suggest (in the same interview) that once a writer gets past the notion that a line simply ends at the "left-hand margin," "new tension [arises] from where you didn't expect it. Removing the secure limit of how far art can take you." Ondaatje was, and continues to be, willing to broach that safety barrier in almost all of his work.

Left margin, right margin, foreground, background — a host

of concepts about literature and film became increasingly important to Ondaatje. This was only partly due to the influence of Nichol's interesting mix of printed word and visual design; many others around Ondaatje were exploring ways to blend picture and language.

Through Kim, Michael was gradually becoming familiar with members of London's visual-arts community. Kim had accepted the post of treasurer of CAR (Canadian Artists' Representation), and she often allowed CAR meetings to be held at their home, invited artists to visit her there, or went to local exhibitions to support their work. Kim and London-based painter Tony Urquhart especially were enthusiastic about the possibilities of CAR, and so they often held extra planning meetings. Urquhart claims that:

Michael got a little jealous when all of Kim's time went into CAR. Some nights — don't forget there was a considerable age difference between Michael and Kim — he'd burst out: "If you're going to have a meeting, I'm leaving. I'm not staying. I'm leaving. Yes I am. I'm leaving." That's the way he talked and acted. Just like a little grumpy boy.

Before some meetings, Michael was calmed down; before others, Kim would just let him leave. "They behaved, sometimes," says Urquhart, "like Kanga and Roo — you know, those characters in *Winnie-the-Pooh*. In fact, her nickname for Michael was Tigger because he was younger and full of energy . . . and boy, when he got going, just like Tigger, he was full of bounce, bounce, bounce."

Three London painters had a considerable impact on Ondaatje's work: Jack Chambers, Robert Fones, and Urquhart. In fact, Ondaatje so liked some of Chambers's work — especially those pieces that had a kind of stark brutality — that he asked permission to use a Chambers painting on the dust jacket of *The Man with Seven Toes*. A fourth, equally well-known artist, Greg Curnoe, might have had some influence on Michael, but, says Urquhart, he and Kim Ondaatje immediately crossed swords. They took to each other like two competitive German shepherds, and that was that. You know, as Michael put it to me one day, Kim never lost an argument — never. [Neither] Michael nor anyone else — in fact I can't think of any person — ever beat her in an argument. In the beginning, I think, [Michael] almost wanted a mother who would run things for him, and Kim sure did. She was a very forceful woman, and she did an awful lot for his career, and it was all to his benefit. . . . That became hard on him later . . . remember, he got married young, very young — at nineteen or so? — to a mature, confident woman who was completely connected, through family, through teaching, through art.

Urquhart also recalls that the Ondaatjes' Piccadilly Street house and their lives in general "were always bedlam." "Kim had a big seven-seater station wagon and she would pack Michael, their kids, my kids, the dogs, and everything else into the car and race us off to one place or another." The Chamberses, Foneses, and Urquharts would often meet. Says Kim, "Since all of us had families, we socialized in nonacademic settings, like picnics, current shows, movies, plays. Michael rarely discussed his own work with the artists, but he was very aware of their art." He expressed considerable interest in Urquhart's work, especially his series of experimental sculpted boxes. One was a so-called Donnelly box, inspired by James Reaney's dramatic trilogy based on the murder of the Donnelly family in Biddulph, near London, Ontario. It was, in particular, a "gory, black box" that Ondaatje couldn't resist, recalls Kim — a "tough image," says Urquhart, made from charred wood (the Donnelly's wooden house was burned to the ground when the family was murdered). Urquhart comments that

Ondaatje was always curious about me . . . my art I mean . . . I was doing these weird things . . . boxes. Michael would approach them intellectually, not physically, sort of scratch his head . . . then look at how I had made the box look burned and charred, like the Donnelly house the night the family was murdered. Then he'd open the box, and inside it was all flesh coloured. It's kind of hard to explain . . . but the box could be opened, and part of it folded down. Once opened, the skin-coloured inside would dominate so that the piece would look like Mrs. Donnelly's bruised knee. She was beaten to death in the final fire. I wanted to get that sense of her inside that house, and Michael couldn't resist looking at it, opening it, closing it. He bought it with the money he got for the Governor General's Award. He's still got it today.

Ondaatje's interest in Urquhart's work led to their collaboration on an anthology of poems and drawings entitled *The Broken Ark: A Book of Beasts* (1971). In his blurb for the book, Ondaatje humorously points out that the text was intended for children, "but gradually we realized that children didn't need it — and that we did." In the tradition of Layton's "The Bull Calf" and Atwood's "The Animals in That Country," *The Broken Ark* asks the reader to identify with the animal, to identify with victimization. Critics had often linked Ondaatje with the gruesome, the shocking, and the violent, and in his blurb for the book he did not hesitate to use these elements in an attempt to prompt such identification on the part of the reader. He wrote: "We want you to imagine yourself pregnant and being chased and pounded to death by snowmobiles. We want you to feel the cage, and the skin and fur on your shoulders."

SHOOTOUT AT THE WESTERN CORRAL

After three years, Ondaatje found that his position as lecturer at the University of Western Ontario was becoming problematic. Although he had declared to the head of the English department that he had no intention of pursuing a Ph.D., and that he preferred to write books of poetry and fiction (and occasional critical work), he did request that the department consider his application for a permanent position. "I think I'm pretty accurate when I say that Kim was behind his choice," says Urquhart. "She felt he had taught well, that his students liked him, that he had a publication record that should give him a solid shot at the job." Moreover, he had already been recognized as a writer of merit by the University of Western Ontario, for in 1967 he had won the poetry award offered by the university, the President's Medal.

Ondaatje, however, knew that his chances of securing the post were slim. His publications, in the main, were not academic or scholarly, but creative, and were known only to the few people who kept up with the Canadian poetry scene. Even his study of Leonard Cohen did not, ultimately, furnish him with scholarly credentials. Many judge *Leonard Cohen* as cogent and insightful; others do not. One critic, Leslie Mundwiler, remarked that it was "somewhat padded with quotation from Cohen's work." Mundwiler granted that Ondaatje's study of Cohen's fiction had its high points, but argued that they were not sustained, and that they reflected the insights of a gifted poet rather than those of a scholar and researcher. Western's English department obviously shared Mundwiler's views (it's important to note, however, that Mundwiler was in no way connected to the controversy that was about to erupt). In retrospect, it might seem mysterious that the university voted not to hire Ondaatje, but the fact is that the nature of his publication record had proven to be an insurmountable obstacle. Ironically, it was announced that Ondaatje had won a major award shortly after the university had officially elected not to renew his contract; but even if the university had known that Ondaatje would receive the Governor General's Award for *Billy the Kid*, their vote would probably not have been swayed.

The Governor General's Award is not given for scholarly achievement, so, at most, the English department and the university itself could only be blamed for firing someone who had suddenly won acclaim for creative writing, not for research.

FIGURE II

Michael Ondaatje in 1971.

During the early sixties, there had been a rapid expansion of southern Ontario universities, and that expansion, in turn, created an increased demand for good, qualified Canadian teachers. Ondaatje met that standard easily when he was hired by the University of Western Ontario to begin teaching in the fall of 1968. But by 1971, when it came time to renew Ondaatje's one-year contract for the third time, university administrations had undergone a major shift in attitude: more and more were insisting on their faculty members having Ph.D.s.

Circumstances forced Ondaatje either to compromise or to leave. He attempted compromise in a letter to his department, but his proposal was rejected. In his formal application for the position of assistant professor, he suggested to the department an alternative arrangement that would allow him both to teach and to write. This request, too, was denied. Kim claims that Michael asked his students not to protest the department's decision, but, because Ondaatje was now a Governor General's Award winner, public reaction was swift. There was an immediate furor. The *London Free Press*, which under normal circumstances would be unlikely to take an interest in standard university hiring practices, seized on the story. Dr. D.S. Hair, the acting head of the English department, told a *Free Press* reporter that the issue was "confidential. If [Ondaatje] wanted to discuss it that's up to him" (see Joe McClelland). A heated editorial entitled "Michael Ondaatje and the uwo" followed three days later. It maintained that the refusal of those involved to discuss the issue openly "suggests that professional jealousy may have figured in the decision."

This attention in the local press forced the usually reticent author to write an open letter to the *London Free Press*. In that letter ("Writer Clarifies Departure from Western Teaching Post"), Ondaatje declared, "My own feelings regarding these decisions I think should remain private," but conceded that his poetry, his short articles, and his manuscript on Leonard Cohen were simply not adequate demonstrations of scholarship. He did not discuss the Governor General's Award, for, as he put it in the letter, "the award I won was not a political one and I had no wish to reduce it to a political weapon." Kim, however, is less reluctant than Michael to point a finger: "Michael was voted the most popular teacher. There was jealousy and resentment among the older faculty because of his youth, talent, and popularity."

In his *Free Press* letter, Ondaatje failed to mention that his students considered him an accomplished teacher. The author of the previously quoted *Free Press* editorial, however, sensed the importance of that fact and challenged the institution's lack of respect for good teaching: "Government, industry and students are now questioning the emphasis placed by educational institutions on the wholesale production of Ph.D. holders." If Ondaatje had gambled that either his reputation as a teacher or his promising career as a poet would win him a job at Western, he lost the bet. If he had counted on his Cohen book to sustain him, he was let down. (Even he had to grant, and he did so in his *Free Press* letter, that in the end it wouldn't do: "I do not consider my Cohen book scholastic as it was not meant to be.") If he had counted on friends for help, he also miscalculated. Although too discrete to name names in the newspaper, Ondaatje made it clear in his poetry that he believed the Western incident was, for some, an invitation to engage in all kinds of backbiting. Who bit whom is questionable, but it's evident that the wrangling left a bad taste in many mouths. Ondaatje published a poem by that name ("A Bad Taste") in *Rat Jelly*:

> Living in London he came closer to the rats.
> There was rat chambers, rat curnoe,
> the cunning rat urquhart, rat reaney and rat fones.
> They travel so sly
> you do not see the teeth
> till in the operating room.

By March 1971, the issue seemed to be dead. Awards came like consolation prizes to Ondaatje, but he was out on the street. In April, he was in the local papers again. This time the *London Free*

FIGURE 12

Michael Ondaatje participates (with Al Purdy and Diane Wakoski) in a University of Toronto poetry workshop.

Press reported that he had won another major award, a Canada Council bursary of four thousand dollars to help sustain him for a year of work and study. He was one of eleven regional winners of this award, as was Kim, who received one to continue her painting. Kim accepted hers, but Michael surprised everyone by turning his down, claiming in the *Free Press* article, entitled "Ondaatje Says He'll Refuse Study Bursary," that he intended "to be teaching next year and therefore [would be] ineligible under the terms of the bursary." By May, that enigmatic comment became clear: Ondaatje had been hired by another university. The *London Free Press*, elated and vindicated for its support of excellent teaching, boldly announced the results: "Award-Winning London Author Appointed to York Teaching Post."

POTSHOTS

Ondaatje, who hated being in the public eye, suddenly could not seem to keep out of the newspapers. While he was widely praised for *Billy the Kid*, it became apparent that he wasn't everyone's darling. One critical voice that Ondaatje couldn't dismiss was Louis Dudek's. This older, well-established writer's assessment of Ondaatje was harsh; he claimed that Ondaatje belonged to a younger generation of authors who were "pretty much of a kind, and not exceptionally well-trained."

Ondaatje was also being attacked, this time indirectly, on another front. He had allowed his work to be printed in a special anthology called *Made in Canada: New Poems of the Seventies* (1971). As one observer noted, what was supposed to be made at home was, in fact, printed in England for Ottawa's Oberon Press. J.A. Harris attacked the anthology in *Canadian Forum* for its "overt commercialism," its "cheapening" of Canadian poetry, even for being a symbol of "editorial trafficking." Ondaatje's determination to keep his private decisions and choices to himself can be best understood in light of the fact that even his simple agreement to have his work included in an anthology could be arbitrarily criticized in the media. Although Ondaatje wasn't actually named in Harris's review, all the anthology's contributors are condemned for their decision to be involved in the project when Harris, speculating about why Irving Layton, Al Purdy, and Leonard Cohen were not included, writes, "I suspect [that these] authors . . . sensed exploitation. . . ."

Ondaatje was also excoriated for having American sympathies. The charge was first levelled by, of all people, John Diefenbaker, a former prime minister of Canada. Diefenbaker "freaked out in true western style," wrote Thomas Gillan in a letter to the *Toronto Star*, and took a "pot shot" at *Billy the Kid*. He complained about the inappropriateness of giving a Canadian prize — the Governor General's Award — to a writer who dealt with an American subject. To make matters worse, Diefenbaker mangled the facts. He blustered, reported the *London Free Press* (in "Diefenbaker Raps Poet"), that the language of the book was "atrocious," and insisted that Canadian historical figures were "every bit as colorful as that what's-his-name in the coonskin hat." Billy the Kid and Davy Crockett were all the same to Diefenbaker. He just wanted it understood that granting an award to Ondaatje was highly inappropriate.

Ondaatje reacted as graciously as possible, while rejoicing a little. Pearl Sheffy Gefen quoted his remarks as he recalled the incident in 1990: "[Diefenbaker] hated [*Billy the Kid*] and thought it was outrageous and disgraceful that it won the award. So he gave a press conference and suddenly my name was plastered on front pages. It was the nicest thing he could have done for me." Ondaatje welcomed such publicity as it could help sell books, but he had not sought it out. At Western, he could have predicted that there would be a shoot-out, but Diefenbaker had given him no warning. Dief the Chief's attack amounted to an ambush. Ondaatje hesitated to ask bluntly why Diefenbaker hadn't read the book well enough to distinguish Davy Crockett from Billy the Kid — to gain points because one reader couldn't tell the difference between a kid in a cowboy hat and a man in a coonskin cap seemed to border on the ludicrous. Tired of the constant calls and requests to comment on the Chief's decision to shoot it out in the press, Ondaatje, quoted in "Diefenbaker Raps Poet," fired back in his own oblique way: "I'm really glad he read it. . . . I think he's great — I really miss him as prime minister." After this parting shot, Ondaatje deliberately retreated into his private life, looking forward to his new job at Glendon College, York University, Toronto.

THE WAY THE POEM MEANS

The Ondaatje family settled, Michael not altogether joyously, into their new home on Wallingford Drive in suburban Don Mills. There Michael devoted his nonteaching time to his writing. The subdivision they lived in was so dull and uniform that he couldn't always recognize his own house, often driving right past it. Finally, Kim remembers, she had two trees planted on the front lawn near the driveway so that Michael would know when to slow down and make the turn.

By the time Ondaatje was offered the job at York, he had received numerous awards and earned a considerable reputation. Although he still didn't have a Ph.D., and had no plans to get one simply for form's sake (certainly with cause after the indignity he had suffered at the University of Western Ontario), he was able to establish a better contract. In fact, the agreement he came to has kept him at York.

At Glendon College he became a member of a faculty that respected imaginative literature and criticism without quarrelling about the distinctions between creative and scholarly writing. Among his colleagues at York were a number of writers, including Barry Callaghan, Miriam Waddington, Don Coles, Hédi Bouraoui, Frank Davey, and Clark Blaise and Bharati Mukherjee (though the latter were not long associated with York). Eli and Ann Mandel were there as well, and they became Ondaatje's friends.

Ondaatje settled in as an assistant professor and began teaching poetry from the perspective of a practising writer. He showed little interest in critical theory. As a poet Ondaatje has always been clearly interested in craftsmanship; as a teacher he resists locking into one particular method of critical analysis. When Solecki (in 1975) asked him "How do you teach poetry?" his response was typical: "[If] I have to teach Ezra Pound's 'Near Perigord,' for example . . . in the middle of the class I'll probably focus on the visual images of the hand and the five ciuies — an image that isn't really spelled out. But it's there all the way through the poem." Ondaatje is evasive when asked to provide technical analysis of his own poetry. Interviewer Jon Pearce tried hard to pin him down:

[PEARCE:] *Let me quote you again. You say that "at universities and schools teachers are preoccupied with certain aspects of content, with themes, with messages." Then you go on to say "that's only about half of poetry." If so, what's the other half?*

[ONDAATJE:] You sound like a lawyer, a criminal lawyer.

Well, I'm not. I'm a school-teacher. But I do happen to have some notes in front of me. I've prepared a bit of a brief so I can try to get you to say what you mean.

Okay. The other half . . . style, technique, the method and movement of the poem. I think William Carlos Williams or someone said he could summarize all the main things about poetry on the back of a postage stamp . . . that's a minor part of the poem. If you read a love poem, well obviously there will be nothing new in a love poem — it's just the way it's said and it's the *way* it's said that makes it suddenly hit you.

*So the question shouldn't be "What *does* the poem mean," but "How *does* a poem mean"?*

Yes, the *way* the poem means.

FIGURE 13

Blue Roof Farm.

Once Pearce obtains this concession, he is so drawn into the debate that he, the interviewer, suddenly becomes the interviewee, and goes on, at some length, to analyse Ondaatje's lines and images and themes himself. Like a good teacher, Ondaatje listens, encourages, comments, and points out that his interviewer's way of reading the poem is "a pretty good interpretation." Ondaatje may resist interpreting his poems, but he openly faces the problems of his creative technique. His sense of a poem, based on modernist and New Critical notions of the poem as a made object, is such that he will look at the product when, and only when, it invites a particular kind of questioning or examination. Once the *way* of a poem exhibits itself, Ondaatje, like any other reader, studies its workings and its imagery. Ondaatje (speaking to Pearce), does recognize the violence of the imagery he uses — it constantly erupts in his work — but claims that he does not employ such violence deliberately:

I don't think I'm conscious of [an image] when I'm writing; I'm not conscious of trying to shock someone when I'm writing with a specific image. That just happens in the process of writing, but I'm not conscious of it while I'm writing it. I don't know what more I can say about that. It's there, and it's obviously part of my style. But I don't think I'm a particularly violent poet, which some people feel I am, and I don't think I'm a grotesque poet, as some people think.

THE SUMMER PLACE

For many years, Kim and Michael Ondaatje spent their summers at a farmhouse they had purchased near Kingston. Because a blue metal roof was installed when an addition to the main house was constructed, it earned the name Blue Roof Farm. Originally, though, it had no name, nor did it have the hot tub, the spacious master bedroom, and the artist's studio it has today. These comforts and amenities were added gradually over the years. The original building was relatively small, with a wonderful, spacious old kitchen, now refurbished; but even if the house had already been renovated and enlarged when the Ondaatjes bought it, it wouldn't have mattered to Michael. He only cared about having a quiet, private place to write, and this he found adjacent to the farmhouse the first time he saw it. The barn became his favourite writing spot. Kim remembers that while Michael was preparing *Billy the Kid*, he worked at a table he had set up in the back corner of the barn, just past the stalls. He became "almost obsessive and superstitious about his routine. He would go to the barn to write from 9:30 until 3:30, and anything in progress was not to be discussed."

Ondaatje may have been enthralled in Billy's brutal world during these long hours, but when he emerged to enjoy get-togethers with friends (these were often held at the farm, and were usually confined to weekends), the mood was anything but serious or brooding or violent. Tom Marshall, who often joined in the festivities, described them in this way: "Parties at the Ondaatjes' summer place might involve enjoyably corny or strenuous games, a volleyball tournament, feeding paperback books to hungry pigs, nude swimming, and late-night (clothed) dancing." Stuart MacKinnon remembers that most of the guests (regulars included himself and his wife, Sally, Fred and Kris Colwell, and Stan and Truus Dragland) had families, so there was, during the first few years, an emphasis on birthday parties and treasure hunts for the kids. The drink and the drugs came later, just before the separations and the divorces.

During their first few summers at the farm, Kim displayed the skills of a stage manager, capably scheduling everything from hot-dog dinners to dances. In later years, her desire to control things seemed to some to slip into meddling; her dominating personality began to weaken her marriage. Many of the marriages of Kim and Michael's friends also began to slide towards collapse. Before the "difficult, heart-wrenching separations — as it is when kids are involved — began" (to quote MacKinnon),

FIGURE 14

Michael Ondaatje and Wallace in 1974.

this group of friends cavorted and played with one another and lived lives that sometimes bordered on mayhem.

Ondaatje, especially, delighted in practical jokes. One of his favourite gags was to reenact silent-movie stunts such as throwing pies in people's faces. Sometimes the timing of the antics, more than the antics themselves, got out of hand. Ondaatje engineered it so that Dragland would slap a cream pie in MacKinnon's face on a day when MacKinnon felt particularly depressed about his separation from Sally. Usually, though, the pranks were harmless. For example, Ondaatje and Marshall demonstrated their rejection of didactic literature by feeding George Orwell's *Animal Farm* to the pigs.

Those who visited the Ondaatjes at Blue Roof Farm — "and" MacKinnon recalls, "there was a constant stream of them: critics, artists, family, friends" — often commented with awe on how life seemed to go on despite the chaos produced by a large brood of children and an equally large brood of dogs. Only two of the dogs, Wallace and Flirt, actually belonged to the Ondaatjes. Wallace, a basset hound, was Michael's favourite pet, and, along with several other tricks, the dog was taught to howl along to "O Canada." He was quite proud of his dog's feat. He even entered him in a local basset-hound contest, and Wallace won first prize for having the longest ears (thirteen inches) of any dog in the Kingston area. After such a victory, Ondaatje couldn't resist, in an interview with the magazine *Manna*, claiming that the violent scenes involving dogs in *Billy the Kid* were inspired by a reading of the introduction to *"How to raise and train your basset."*

Although not filmed at Blue Roof Farm, Ondaatje's comic short film entitled *Carry on Crime and Punishment* captures the spirit of comic lightness that characterized the family parties he and Kim held there. In the film (shot at Loughborough Lake, where the Ondaatjes had rented a place called Brown Cottage the summer before they bought Blue Roof Farm), Ondaatje cast family and friends, including the mob of children with which he liked to surround himself. The plot centred on the dognapping of Wallace. In the annual League of Canadian Poets members catalogue, Ondaatje declared the film to be "a 4 minute moral adventure." The lead roles were played by Marshall and Mac-Kinnon — dressed like bums out of Beckett and hobbling through the countryside. It is a fast-motion, slapstick, Keystone Cops comedy that attempts to recreate the flickering effect of early silent films. The tramps kidnap the dog and the children chase them all over the place, until, finally, they are brought to justice.

Carry on Crime and Punishment is a testimony to the friendship that existed within this band of writers. It particularly demonstrates the bond between MacKinnon and Ondaatje, who, since their *Quarry* days, had worked together, read and responded to each other's work — and, most importantly, had enjoyed doing it. When Ondaatje wasn't behind the camera, he was reading MacKinnon's manuscript version of *The Intervals*: "I told [Mac-Kinnon] it was 'fantastic,'" he said to Solecki (in 1975). "He rewrote the whole thing again. I said, 'This is even better. Don't change a word.' And I think he's rewritten it once again since then." MacKinnon summarizes their relationship in those years:

I knew him best from around 1968 to 1978, when he was at that most vulnerable time for a writer: early development. But also this is sometimes the writer's most confident time, as no one has taken really hard punches at you in print. I'd say he was very thin-skinned, easily upset, tense, high-strung, nervous, afraid, like most writers, but also bursting with energy. That's what drove him through.

No one who knew Ondaatje then (or who knows him now), can ever forget "his charm, his anger, his love of games, practical jokes, team sports," maintains MacKinnon. To MacKinnon, Ondaatje, as a poet, was the "preeminent (lowercase) postmodern. . . . His option . . . nihilism."

When elated, Ondaatje raced friends to the farm in his dilapidated white Volvo. "He drove it for about eleven years," recollects Kim, "even with one window badly broken. He never washed it, and he kept it until it wouldn't move anymore." When depressed, wondering if it was all worth the effort, he indulged himself in the privacy the vehicle provided, as he reveals in a poem (published in *Black Moss* in 1969) called "Thoughts in a Volvo: Or, Why Rex Reed Hasn't Interviewed Canadian Poets Yet." Work was not the only aspect of life that troubled Ondaatje.

Regardless of the personal bonds he had forged, he was already sensing the inevitable collapse of friendships and intimacies. He recorded that precognition in a poem revealingly titled "We're at the Graveyard" (in *Rat Jelly*). But the separations and divorces, the ruptured friendships, would come later. From 1969 to 1972 there was more fulfilment than failure. If shooting *Carry on Crime and Punishment* was just plain fun for Ondaatje, the work of editing it was a valuable rehearsal for his next project. Ondaatje began to plan a new film, and this time he would be working with Paul Thompson, the founder of Theatre Passe Muraille.

THE CLINTON SPECIAL:
LIFE INTO MYTH

Paul Thompson had been working on a project called *The Farm Show*, a theatre production without walls. The aim was to mingle actor with audience; the result was a "happening," not a staged product. Ondaatje and Thompson had already collaborated on a dramatic version of *The Man with Seven Toes*, and they were discussing possible ways of presenting *Billy the Kid* on the stage, but for the moment Ondaatje was intrigued by the idea of catching Thompson's living theatre on celluloid. He would do this, from 1972 to 1973, in a film called *The Clinton Special*.

The project was launched after Ondaatje had seen *The Farm Show*, which Paul Thompson had developed with the actors of the Theatre Passe Muraille. At first, Ondaatje said to Solecki (in 1975), he had considered drama "a dead art," but he soon saw all the possibilities that were in the theatre; the whole of documentary drama, the possibilities of finding your own mythology in your own landscape; and it was, again, a very freeing thing, for me, in the same way that Nichol's aesthetics had been.

His imagination was fired when he heard that Thompson was planning to go "on a tour of the auction barns and back to the same farming community [Clinton County, Ontario] in which the play had originated. . . . I was also very interested in the reactions of the people to seeing themselves on stage. . . ." A similar notion would strike a chord in Ondaatje about ten years later, when he undertook to write *Running in the Family*: like his own family history, which was part myth, part fact, part disguise, part self-revelation, the whole *Farm Show* venture was a way of seeing oneself. It was self-projection through art.

As Ondaatje explained to Solecki (in 1975), a large part of *The Clinton Special* was filmed during a four-night run of performances that were part of the company's 1972 tour; additional footage — interviews with the actors — was shot in the spring of 1973; in the summer of that year, Ondaatje and his crew returned to Clinton to meet with the actual subjects of the play and to film their homes and the landscape. The cameramen were Bob Carney and Bob Fresco. Ondaatje had little money for the project — only about five hundred dollars — so he applied for and received an Ontario Arts Council award. He was granted only three thousand dollars, barely enough to pay for the travel costs, the equipment, and the film (processing would have to be paid by another source). They borrowed cameras where they could. Later, Ondaatje told Solecki, that would lead to some furious quarrels about who owed whom how much and for what: "One of the cameras got broken and in the auction barn, for example, a lot of the stuff from the barn was ruined."

After shooting the tour, they filmed interviews with the individual actors. In August of 1972 they went to Clinton to meet the people on whom the *Farm Show* characters were based. Of major concern to Ondaatje, as it had been when he was filming *Sons of Captain Poetry*, was to avoid creating (he remarked to Solecki in the same interview) "the CBC kind of documentary which knows what it's going to say before the actual filming begins." Once all the material was on the reels, Ondaatje began to work at splicing sections together into a unified whole. (The alternating use of colour and black and white in the film was due largely to budgetary, as opposed to aesthetic, concerns.) Even though the film has never achieved commercial success, its importance cannot be underestimated. *Coming through Slaughter* (1976) and *Running in the Family* (1982) were, in some ways, products of *The Clinton Special* and Ondaatje's other film projects. Ondaatje explains that "Making the documentaries influenced my writing, just as my writing influenced the way I made the documentaries. I don't want to make films that are part of a genre someone else has invented. I want to write movies related to what I'm writing" (see Gefen). The creative process was, as it is in every Ondaatje project, a method of gradual discovery; the forming and shaping could take place only after the material had been gathered. "With the actual editing," he continued to Solecki (in 1975), "that's when the director moves in. That's when you decide the film's structure. You remake the whole film."

Ondaatje's sense of technique in *The Clinton Special* was remarkably close to that evident in *Billy the Kid*, with its vivid imagery: the camera had to be static, the scenes dominated by a photo effect, the tension between stasis and kinesis had to prevail. "I wanted that sense throughout the film," he elaborated in the same interview, "that each shot would almost be a static photograph. Thus throughout the film the camera doesn't move very much at all. . . ." Ondaatje was pleased that the overall effect of the movie is to make the viewer feel estranged. The odd dynamic of human subjects watching themselves portrayed by actors gives rise to a fascinating blend of fact and fiction, reality and artifice, life and mythology.

A rather odd feature of *The Clinton Special* is the inclusion of an isolated wanderer, Charlie Wilson, a manic figure who lived in the community but who was removed from its aims and ideals. Ondaatje was interested in him even before he had formulated his plan to film *The Farm Show*. When, prompted by his ever-present documentary impulse, Ondaatje tried to find photographs of Wilson to use in his film, he failed to turn up a single picture of the eccentric loner, and he had to resign himself to using a still of an abandoned cabin where Wilson had once spent a winter. The oddness of Wilson's behaviour and character, as well as the community's reaction to him, Ondaatje found compelling. He was fascinated by the way in which the obsessive talk of a community can turn a misfit into a living legend. More interesting still was the fact that Wilson would, on occasion, enter the homes of those who had mythologized him, Ondaatje goes on to tell Solecki, "to watch Bonanza, you know, totally unaware that he himself is a myth and that Bonanza is third rate mythology." Thompson remarks in the film that "You have to create your own mythology," a line Ondaatje particularly liked. Underlying *The Clinton Special* is Ondaatje's belief that by dramatizing real lives, without excessive reshaping, an artist can make the everyday seem extraordinary, even mythical.

The Clinton Special, however, was not Ondaatje's alone, and he had to make compromises. He would have preferred a darker, more brooding film, and he would also have chosen a radically different ending, one in which (he told Solecki in 1975)

> After the applause at the end everyone stands up and we cut to old Mrs. Lobb who proceeds to tell us a long, long, long, very long story of some wedding; the film runs out but the sound keeps on and on . . . that would have made the point as to where the source of the play and the film lies, in the raw material of stories told to the actors.

He was not granted this wish because Thompson, who had initially worked out the play as a "happening," wished to keep to the original design of the work, but he did get to pay tribute to one of his favourite film directors, Alfred Hitchcock.

FIGURE 15

Michael Ondaatje.

Hitchcock was famous for appearing, usually for only a few seconds, in each of his films. Ondaatje resolved to leave that kind of personal mark on *The Clinton Special*. Much of the action is set in a barn temporarily converted into a theatre. The farmers and their families enter noisily, dressed in their Sunday best, eagerly anticipating the spectacle. Suddenly Ondaatje appears. He is clearly nervous and self-conscious. Dressed in blue jeans and a plaid shirt, handsome and well built, he might be one of the local farmhands, though one somehow doubts that this man has ever lugged bales of hay or shovelled manure. He strides quickly across the barn floor, looks at the camera for a second, approaches it hastily, then disappears behind it, ready to direct the action. It's a short sequence, but a revealing one. It's the moment when art and life blend, the moment when Ondaatje joins his subjects: he acts himself as they act themselves.

THE NEXT ALTER EGO

While filming *The Clinton Special* in 1972, Ondaatje began writing the initial drafts of a novel that would later be called *Coming through Slaughter*, but the film was anything but a distraction. It enabled him to experiment with mixing fact and fiction and to observe the results; this activity only enhanced the creative energy he brought to bear on his experimental novel. *Coming through Slaughter*, however, required over four years of hard writing and rewriting, and it must have been a relief for Ondaatje to work occasionally on either the film or the collection of poetry, called *Rat Jelly*, that he completed in 1973.

As he awaited the release of *Rat Jelly*, he and Kim took a trip to New Orleans and Baton Rouge. Since he had discovered that Buddy Bolden — the Black American jazz cornetist who reached the peak of his career at the turn of the century — went mad while marching in a Louisiana parade, Ondaatje had been researching Bolden's life. Initially, he simply read the material he acknowledges at the end of *Coming through Slaughter* (such as William

Russell and Stephen Smith's "New Orleans Music," and Martin Williams's *Jazz Masters of New Orleans*). As the first sections of a possible new work began to take shape in his mind and on paper, he and Kim left for Louisiana to do further research and to absorb the geography of Bolden's life. Most of the details of Bolden's experience and environment, as they are recreated in the novel, are derived from the material Ondaatje studied in the local archives, such as period photographs, newspaper clippings, tape digests of interviews, and books, including histories of jazz. When he finally arrived in New Orleans, Mark Witten writes in "Billy, Buddy, and Michael," Ondaatje made a point of "coming through the hamlet of Slaughter, as Bolden did 70 years ago, [and then] visit[ing] the East Louisiana State Hospital in Jackson, about 50 miles north of Baton Rouge."

The hospital in Jackson, a mental institution, was "The only place I was really interested in going to," Ondaatje recalls in the same article. There Bolden passed the final twenty-four years of his life. Curious about the building, Ondaatje met with hospital superintendent Lionel Gremillion, who recounted its history. The Ondaatjes also made side trips to such sites as the Holtz Cemetery.

The recorded facts pertaining to Bolden's life, Ondaatje has stressed in several interviews, scarcely fill a page, and one short visit to Bolden's home territory would hardly allow for a profound understanding of the geographical and social forces that shaped his life. Such a trip would merely provide Ondaatje with a sense of the place. More valuable to him than geographic impressions was the material he found in the jazz archives of Tulane University, material he could easily adopt and adapt. He freely changed facts and altered dates. As Witten goes on to report, Ondaatje felt the novel should be a statement about an artist, not a true history of a man, so "Why," he asked, should he "hold facts sacred when they can be more valuable as clues, beginnings to truth?" Ondaatje's aim was to use the legend of one particular artist and to transform it into a contemporary mythology. Even "The landscape of the book is a totally mental landscape. It really was a landscape of names and rumours. Somebody tells you a rumour and that becomes a truth."

The test of the novel's success came at the launching party held in the theatre at Toronto's A Space. Established in 1970, A Space is an artist-run centre with a multidisciplinary program. Under the direction of Victor Coleman, who along with Ondaatje was also an editor at Coach House Press, A Space had sponsored literary readings and performances by such writers as William Burroughs, John Giorno, the Four Horsemen and, of course, Michael Ondaatje. Because he was uncertain about what kind of reception *Coming through Slaughter* would receive, Ondaatje introduced it to his audience as a "soup." He felt he had to offer a warning about the novel's mix of rumour and fact, as it was likely that many would be puzzled by its form. *Coming through Slaughter* was to be understood as a poetic novel based on the life of Buddy Bolden and constructed with impressionistic fragments and images. A Space was the ideal place for Ondaatje to serve his soup, for the listeners who assembled there were not only sympathetic and knowledgeable, but also familiar with experimental writing.

As the publication of *Coming through Slaughter* neared, Ondaatje must have realized that readers, now more than ever, would want to know more about the man behind such puzzling and violent works as this novel and *Billy the Kid*. Urjo Kareda, who worked with Ondaatje for five years on a revival of the stage version of *Billy the Kid*, stated the issue directly to *Globe and Mail* reporter Val Ross: "There's this courteous, controlled man with pale eyes. And there's violence in book after book. It's unresolved. And mysterious." The search for the man behind the narrator was on.

Ondaatje was now cast as the quiet, gentle, unassuming professor who, once a pen is in his hand, turns to shocking imagery and violent language. The paradox was exploited by journalists who typecast him as the poetic gunslinger, the jazz-mad professor, the embodiment of gentle brutality — a living, breathing oxymoron. After interviewing Kim and Michael Ondaatje for a

Saturday Night article, Kareda claimed that "The startling passage early in *Slaughter*, in which an enraged Bolden, seated across from his wife, knocks out a window with his open palm and then finds 'his hand miraculously uncut,' was a recreation of an incident in the Ondaatjes' own kitchen." Kim, when asked about the incident, both defuses the mystery and intensifies it at the same time. She admits that she recognizes events from their own lives throughout Michael's work, but she only vaguely remembers that such a window-breaking incident occurred, and can't recall what triggered it:

> Michael often telescoped events and happenings, collapsing different episodes and actions . . . of our lives and of others'. The name Livingstone in *Billy the Kid* is the name of his friend, Ken Livingstone. But Michael, like all writers, transformed things.

Like Michael, Kim leaves readers to wonder whether the author's voice in the novel has revealed more than he cares to admit. Speaking of the protagonist of *Coming through Slaughter*, Ondaatje said "You never know what someone is thinking. . . . It's really horrifying. . . . You know Bolden is completely sane and refuses to talk to us" (quoted by Witten). Ondaatje, like his own protagonist, is also "sane," and he, too, refuses to "talk to us." It's not the violent persona, but the silent, secretive one that seems closer to Ondaatje.

The traditional novel has always brought the reader to an epiphany, to a moment of insight and understanding. Ondaatje's novel shoves the reader into moments of baffling fictional confession. Bolden's plight is Ondaatje's own. Ondaatje admits this, though he has altered Bolden's inner experience to create what he calls (records Witten) "a parable of the 20th-century artist. Everybody at one point writes *A Portrait of the Artist*. Their version of it." But parable is not autobiography; only some of the facts of his life, as he writes in his final notes in *Coming through Slaughter*, have been "polished to suit the truth of fiction."

Ondaatje was unsure how reviewers would respond to *Coming through Slaughter*, but he needn't have been. It was named co-winner of the 1976 *Books in Canada* First Novel Award, along with Ian McLachlan's *The Seventh Hexagram*. These two writers, who had written two radically different novels — one an experimental soup and one a very slick, well-paced spy narrative — accepted their shared award on 12 June at the Royal York Hotel in Toronto.

ONDAATJE AND KROETSCH

On a break from writing and editing in 1977, Ondaatje went on a canoeing trip with Robert Kroetsch on the Red Deer River in Alberta. The trip was not only a break for Ondaatje from both his teaching and his public-reading schedule, but also a chance to have some intense discussion about his most recent project — his first feature-length screenplay of another writer's work. It was to be based on Kroetsch's novel *Badlands*, and would be called "The William Dawe Badlands Expedition 1916." (A film was never produced, but the screenplay was published in a 1983 issue of *Descant*.)

Ondaatje hadn't made a movie since *The Clinton Special* in 1972, but the medium still captured his imagination. In fact, he has often joked that *Billy the Kid* was really the movie he couldn't afford to shoot. Now that he was an established writer, he laughingly revealed why he had let filmmaking fall by the wayside. In a 1984 interview, he told Solecki:

> my main image of making movies is still carrying heavy cans of film through railroad stations. Writing is obviously more difficult and complex but at least you decide where to go, what to carry. Someone should work on this whole question of laziness. I hear that William Carlos Williams turned from art to writing because easels were cumbersome.

This explanation, of course, has little basis in fact: Ondaatje would always be ready to face the rigours of movie making. He had important reasons for thinking of Kroetsch's novel in cinematic terms. He was determined to transform *Coming through Slaughter* into a screenplay, and realized that Kroetsch's novel was as complicated and fluid as his own. If he undertook to script *Badlands* first, it would afford him the opportunity to practise preparing such material for the screen in a relatively objective and detached manner. It would be a far greater challenge for him to effect such a transformation with work to which he was so intimately connected.

Ondaatje, after working with the Kroetsch material, did turn *Coming through Slaughter* into a screenplay. He told Gefen that the "Slaughter script was commissioned, so I wrote it. It didn't go very far, but it may happen in the future." Kim's memory of the incident is slightly different. She believes that the script of *Coming through Slaughter* showed serious screen potential, for Ondaatje's New York agent managed to sell the movie rights for a handsome sum. Kim comments that, if she remembers correctly, "Michael was able to purchase a cottage on the Skootamatta River, near Madoc, Ontario, with the money he derived from the screen rights." Neither Ondaatje nor anyone else ever did take on the job of wrestling the script into a movie.

PERSONAL RECOGNITION, AND A LITTLE HELP FOR SOME FRIENDS

Ondaatje's reputation had increased considerably during this time, and in 1977 he became part of a trio of poets — the others were Earle Birney and P.K. Page — selected by the League of Canadian Poets to take part in an exchange program with British poets C.H. Sisson, Geoffrey Hill, and Brian Patten. On 23 September all six poets read at Harbourfront in Toronto. They were hosted by Greg Gatenby. The following day, the group flew to London to stage a second reading. A young, poor Ondaatje had left England in 1952, and now the Department of External Affairs was paying for his return visit. He made light of the affair by

FIGURE 16

Michael Ondaatje celebrates winning the Governor General's Award for There's a Trick with a Knife I'm Learning to Do.

FIGURE 17

*Earle Birney presents the Governor
General's Award to Michael Ondaatje.*

claiming, Kim says, that on this visit "his mother suddenly discovered that her son had become a poet, though she obviously knew that long before."

Creating that little tale about his mother may have helped him to push his legend along, but the fact is that after his return Ondaatje began, in a sense, to see his personal and professional mission in a new light. He had always admired the poetry of the expatriate American Ezra Pound, but not just the craftsmanship it displayed. What Ondaatje especially admired was Pound's utter dedication to writing and writers. He was impressed by the fact that Pound had taken upon himself the responsibility of fostering other writers wherever and whenever he could. Pound is best known for encouraging T.S. Eliot and James Joyce, and helping them to publish. Pound was the kind of figure that fascinated Ondaatje: extremely intelligent, capable, dedicated, even obsessed. Like Buddy Bolden, Pound went mad and spent many years locked up in an institution. It would be utterly wrong to suggest that Ondaatje idolized Pound. However, as a student at Bishop's and Queen's he had been struck by the tremendous energy Pound had directed towards the literary cause.

Having matured as an artist, and having attained a certain level of success, Ondaatje, like Pound, dedicated himself more than ever to literature, his own and that of others. With increasing dedication, he read, edited, and encouraged various writers — Christopher Dewdney, Lola Lemire Tostevin, and Jane Urquhart, to name but a few. Joe Rosenblatt has told me that after he had requested financial assistance from the Canada Council, he discovered that Ondaatje, without even being asked, had supported his project.

Kim maintains that behind the scenes "Michael was always willing to support writers and literary projects." When influential Canadian poetry editor Alan Crawley died, Ondaatje proposed that an Alan Crawley memorial fund be established to sponsor an annual award for a first book of poetry by a young poet. Robert Enright, the editor of *CV/II*, immediately ran Ondaatje's notice about his proposal in that journal, and offered help, but it is clear that the project was initiated by Ondaatje.

After achieving recognition as a Canadian writer, Ondaatje also put even greater effort into the editorial work he did for Coach House Press. When asked by Solecki (in 1984) if he saw connections between his writing and his editing, he responded, "Well, most writers exchange work with each other anyway. I reacted to Daphne Marlatt's *Zocalo* and *How Hug a Stone* and she's helped me often with my books." Although he treats the subject in an offhand way, the fact is that Ondaatje, over the years, has shown considerable commitment to his fellow writers. He admired Sharon Thesen's books, invited her to submit her work to the press, and then saw her submissions through to publication. He has supported the work of numerous writers by reviewing it (as he did for Roy Kiyooka), by reading and commenting on it in manuscript form (as he did for Eli Mandel), and by seeing it through the press (as he did for Stan Dragland with *Peckertracks: A Chronicle* [1978]).

His literary friendships, Kim remarks, were always of a similar nature: they were intense relationships based on the creative process, writing, editing. "Michael always had lots of energy for helping, guiding, assisting others." He began to immerse himself even more deeply in Canadian writing, and rarely sought public recognition for his contributions. His impact on Canadian writing, therefore, must be considered in two ways: he has, as an active writer, played a significant role in shaping the Canadian imagination; he has, through his encouragement and support of other writers, helped to enrich the canon of Canadian literature.

THE ELIMINATION DANCE

Ondaatje has always had a keen sense of humour about virtually everything, even literature. His dark, cutting humour is displayed with special clarity in a small chapbook filled with cryptic statements called *Elimination Dance*. Stan Dragland and Don McKay, attracted by the comic tone of the manuscript, published the booklet in 1978 at Nairn Publishing in Ilderton, Ontario. The work is a series of brittle remarks dedicated to "All those bad poets who claim me as an early influence." Some of the humour reveals Ondaatje's exhaustion, and some his penchant for "eliminating" the pretentiousness so often associated with art and artists. The original orange chapbook was updated and reprinted as a glossy paperback subtitled *Traveller's Edition* with a cover photo of Ondaatje, presumably drunk, out cold, face flat on the table. Expressions of irreverent literary humour have always been part of Ondaatje's nature, and *Elimination Dance* provides a rare example of this impulse in print.

The year the first edition of *Elimination Dance* was published was also a year of personal discovery for Ondaatje. In January of 1978, accompanied by Kim and their children, he travelled to Sri Lanka for a five-month visit with his sister, Gillian, and various relatives. During this extended sojourn, he immersed himself in his family, his past, and his memories of the father from whom he had been separated.

By 1979, however, Kim and Michael's marriage was under strain, as once Michael's parents' had been. He travelled to China alone, and then, on his return to Canada, accepted an invitation to attend a writers' conference in Hawaii. While Ondaatje was at the conference, Kim travelled as far as Alaska, taking photos of churches for her book *Small Churches in Canada* (1982). When she arrived home, Michael was still in Hawaii. Two weeks later, she says, as she was packing her photographic equipment for another trip, "Michael suddenly called to say that he was tired and exhausted and so planned to extend his trip into a short holiday." What Kim neither knew nor suspected was that Michael was not alone. In Hawaii he had met a woman named Linda Spalding, who was living in Honolulu. Within the year Ondaatje (on leave from Glendon College) would accept a one-year post as creative writer at the University of Hawaii at Manoa.

Linda Spalding was born on 25 June 1943 in Topeka, Kansas, the daughter of Jacob Alan Dickinson (an attorney) and his wife, Edith Virginia. Linda married Philip Spalding in 1963 while she was a student in Kansas. She completed her B.A. at the University of Colorado in 1965. The couple had two daughters. Linda completed her graduate studies at the University of Hawaii at Manoa in 1972, and later that year she divorced Philip. Her career was in child care, and from 1972 to 1982 she worked as a social-services administrator for low-income families in Hawaii. She was also a program-development manager for Honolulu's public television station. Linda was deeply interested in the arts, especially literature, and part of her job was to conduct interviews with writers for various television programs. She used some of the interview scripts in her first book, entitled *Interchange*, a collection of essays and interviews on regionalism and ethnicity.

Michael and Kim's marriage ended after Michael's 1980 trip to Hawaii. They agreed to a legal separation rather than a divorce. Their Don Mills home was sold, as were many of the artifacts they had collected over the years, and the profits covered their immediate costs. Michael moved into a house on Major Street in Toronto with Linda Spalding and her two children. Kim moved to Blue Roof Farm, which, over the years, she has converted into a charming bed-and-breakfast guest house. Like Michael's mother, Kim had to learn to make an independent living by taking in lodgers. Michael embarked on a new life with another talented, creative woman, though this time his partner was a writer and editor rather than a painter, photographer, and filmmaker. While Linda was completing the draft of her first novel, *Daughters of Captain Cook*, she and Michael began to edit a publication called *Brick: A Journal of Reviews*.

THE PAIN OF SECULAR LOVE

The disintegration of Kim and Michael's marriage was gradual and painful, and their separation was not made public for several years. Shortly before the separation, in August 1980, Kim worked on a film entitled *Where Bittersweet Grows*, the first in a planned trilogy. That Michael's decision to leave might have devastating

FIGURE 18

Kim Ondaatje, filmmaker.

FIGURE 19

Linda Spalding.

consequences for her is probably best revealed by her own comment to reporter David Pulver, who spoke to her about the making of the film and about her career as a painter and filmmaker. Kim conceded, "I couldn't do this work [filmmaking] if I ever found myself in the position of having to support myself and the children." At the time she made this statement she had no idea of how soon her life would change.

If hers changed suddenly, Michael's changed slowly — very slowly. Many of the poems he wrote through 1979 and 1980 are filled with expressions of pain and guilt, though few were published until 1984, when *Secular Love* appeared. If one had been able to look over his shoulder as he struggled to transcribe his feelings, one would likely have seen, immediately, how deeply troubled he was that his marriage was coming to an end. As Ken Adachi wrote in his review of *Secular Love*, "Dwelling on absences, following obsessive private rituals, working out dramas of loss and disaffection," many of the poems "baffle at first sight. They seem to gravitate towards deep, dark, sometimes surreal, places." The poems read, Adachi continues, "like a commentary on [Ondaatje's] more recent adult experiences, the pain and turbulence of a marriage break-up and a new relationship ('[I]n the midst of love for you / my wife's suffering / anger in every direction')."

His relationship with Linda forced Ondaatje more deeply into himself than ever before, and the personal reassessment he was undergoing gave rise to his most private, difficult poem: "Tin Roof," published in *Secular Love*. It is an oblique, confessional account of the tensions he embraced and endured after his marriage had collapsed. Much of the enigmatic poem centres on subtle nuances of fact and emotion, understood in their fullest sense only by the poet himself. The references to the poet Rainer Maria Rilke, though, seem less cryptic when the reader knows that Kim, to celebrate their marriage in 1964, had given Michael an edition of Rilke's poetry.

"Tin Roof" was written about a period when Ondaatje (like his father before him) was alone on an island (Hawaii) far from his children, and capable of communicating with them only by telephone or letter. Family was becoming more and more important to Ondaatje. He was increasingly haunted by Ceylon, at least by his separation from it, and, of course, by his separation from his father, his wife, his son, and his daughter. A few years earlier, Mark Witten reports in "Billy, Buddy, and Michael," he had realized that "In a way, I'm a very displaced person. I really envy roots," and by 1980 he would envy family stability profoundly. It is no coincidence, then, that "Tin Roof" was written while Ondaatje was shaping *Running in the Family*. His wrestling with love, and with his sense of where he belonged, was becoming more and more urgent.

CREATING A FAMILY CHRONICLE

Only through his writing could Ondaatje, to some degree, come to terms with the loss of the family he'd had and discover the family he'd never quite had. With *Running in the Family*, he immersed himself in this complex and arduous task. As always, he at first allowed the material to shape itself, but later took control of the final form. Ondaatje finally showed the manuscript of *Running in the Family* to his friends Dennis Lee, bp Nichol, Ken Livingstone, and Stan Dragland. He also showed it to Daphne Marlatt, and paid special tribute to her contribution. He told Solecki (in 1984) that Marlatt had remarked that one chapter was "a retelling of a fairy tale and she thought it was awful — so that went." Marlatt had only recently returned from a visit to Penang, Southeast Asia, where she had lived for six years with her family before moving to Vancouver in 1951. She was writing about her journey, and so was an extremely sensitive reader for Ondaatje, and understood some of the feelings he was experiencing. Sections of their two narratives, in fact, appeared together in a 1979 issue of the *Capilano Review*.

It was imperative, however, that Ondaatje gauge the reactions of an even more important group of readers. Because he was

FIGURE 20

Michael Ondaatje in 1979.

writing a type of family chronicle, he felt bound by certain responsibilities that would not have arisen had he been writing straight fiction. In composing *Billy the Kid* and *Coming through Slaughter* he had been able to wreak havoc with the facts, to mould them into the shape he desired, but now, working on *Running in the Family*, he could distort the truth only at the risk of injuring members of his family. Although he had already carefully consulted his relatives and recorded their impressions, he still sent drafts to all those involved, and solicited their views and comments. He was certain that any family member who was hurt or offended by the story he had constructed would have told him so directly. Their general approval of his admittedly fictional rendition of their lives was probably best expressed by Christopher, who, in *The Man-Eater of Punanai*, wrote:

> The great achievement of my brother Michael's superb book *Running in the Family* was to re-create the world of the Ondaatjes, Sproules, de Sarams, even though he had been too young to remember it in its heyday. Through interviews and research, by travelling back to Ceylon in reality and in his imagination, he painstakingly assembled the pieces of the puzzle that had been the Somerset Maugham existence of Colombo high society at the cusp, just before it collapsed into nothingness. And he got it right: the mood, the irresponsibility, the jazz, the frivolity, and the ultimate senselessness.

For Michael, however, the book is the final result of an act of love. "I just had to say to myself," he told Solecki (in 1984), "that I thought I was writing the book with enough love, that if it was me it would be ok. And that in the end was the final test for me." For a different view, one could turn to Ondaatje's unnamed aunt in the United States, who is probably more mythical than real; for her the book evoked, Ondaatje says in the same interview, a world of "Drinking, drinking, drinking; no one is making love." After the publication of *Running in the Family*, Ondaatje again found himself boxed in by the media. Like Earle Birney, who was often constantly asked if he had killed the title character of his poem "David" (in which the narrator confesses to the mercy killing of his friend), Ondaatje was now regularly asked if he had written a biography. He has always denied this, emphasizing that the realism in the book is of tone or mood or spirit, not of historical detail. When pestered with questions about how much of his real self is revealed in the book (as a character in the story, he plays only a small role, and is usually confined to the background), and about the degree to which the portrayal of his family's "madness" is based on fact, he cuts his interlocutors off by saying, "Anyone can sit down and write a book about their family, and they'll discover they're all crazy. Including the writer" (see Gefen). But to the serious listener — in this case interviewer Linda Hutcheon — Ondaatje will elaborate the philosophy behind the characterization in the novel:

> It would have been very easy to make the whole thing an ironic or even sarcastic look at the generation. But why bother? When characters in books are "lesser" than the writer, there seems to be a great loss in the subtleties and truths being discovered or discussed. Obviously the politics of the time is important. But it *is* a book about a family. Also the thing about writing is that you want to represent or make characters who are believable, who are fully rounded, and that stops you from making them just politically good or politically vicious. I'm more interested, I guess, in making people as believable and complex and intricate as possible.

Running in the Family is to be read as the record of the narrator's quest to find the roots of his own imagination in the details of his birth, his family, his inheritance. After all, the book was written at a time when Ondaatje, like his own father before him, was experiencing the powerful desires, moods, and tensions that would separate him from his wife and children. The book portrays the father not only as an idea, as an image of love and fidelity and responsibility, but also as a figure who has abandoned and betrayed. Ondaatje had to understand this father and forgive him in an imaginative encounter, for there could be no other form of reconciliation.

The differences between imaginative insights and actual fact in *Running in the Family* are addressed directly by Christopher Ondaatje. He notes that Michael's presentation of Mervyn Ondaatje makes the man seem dazzling and alluring, and this portrait stands in stark contrast to his own memory of his father: ". . . I had been deeply involved with that man, and I had had to grapple with his demons, which never seemed either romantic or amusing." Michael describes the children wailing at their drunken father's bedside; Christopher remembers helping his inebriated father "to bed at ten in the morning." Michael interprets his father nearly driving off a cliff as a demonstration of Mervyn's idiosyncratic desire for mastery and control. Christopher, a survivor of the incident, remembers it this way:

> I had been in the car with him and my two sisters when he had driven to the edge of a steep precipice. I had had to make the decision to leave the car, with my sisters in it, to get help. In Michael's book this incident became rather light-hearted, as my sisters argued over who was the heavier and who could get out to fetch help without sending the car plunging off the road. At the time there was only terror.

The question of why Mervyn Ondaatje failed so miserably in life haunts the narrative of *Running in the Family*, and is considerably elucidated in Christopher's insightful memoir:

> Though he could be kind and lenient to a fault, he could also be a tyrant. Though he could be very loving, he always expected things to be done his way. And though he could be vulnerable, he sometimes reduced everything to rubble with his thoughtlessness, his drunkenness, his borrowing, and his irresponsibility towards his business and, sometimes, his family. At root, I suspect that, despite his very attractive qualities and his aristocratic demeanour, he lacked self-esteem.

FIGURE 21

Michael Ondaatje edits Love Clinic *in 1991.*

Michael fictionalizes other relatives in an effort to elevate the local and the particular to the status of myth — a type of myth that generates a distinct impression of realism. His grandmother, Lalla, for example, was hardly the romantic figure he presents her to be. She was more likely to be found gambling than plucking flowers from neighbourhood gardens, and she died rather unromantically of alcohol poisoning: "She and her brother had been out drinking," writes Christopher, "and Lalla simply never woke up." Michael's account of his family, in other words, emphasizes the nuances, the mood of the time; Christopher's attempts to adhere to the cold, hard facts. Michael's indisputably imaginative re-creation of a period stands in stark contrast to his older brother's reportage. Their narratives reflect their distinct temperaments and their divergent reasons for stressing some facts while embellishing others.

Ironically, the tendency of people in general to confuse fact and fiction did, for several hours, terrorize Christopher Ondaatje. It happened when Ken Adachi, the well-known *Toronto Star* writer and book reviewer, committed suicide in 1989. Christopher, visiting Sri Lanka at the time, heard that "an Ondaatje had killed himself in Canada." After hours of frantic telexing and phoning, Christopher was able to reach Michael and lay his fears to rest. Upon returning to Canada, he discovered that "Michael's name had been confused in the transmission, mistaken for that of . . . Ken Adachi, who had indeed tragically killed himself" (see *The Man-Eater of Punanai*). For Christopher, this discovery led to the realization that the boundaries between gossip and rumour and fact are often as blurred in life as they are in his brother's fiction.

POLITICS AND ETHNICITY: THE STRUGGLE TO BE UNDERSTOOD

The issue of verisimilitude in *Running in the Family* was, at the same time, provoking reactions from a very different quarter.

Canadian journalists and reviewers of South Asian origin took exception to Ondaatje's emphasis on his wealthy family's extreme eccentricity. Ondaatje was charged with ignoring the pressing social and political issues of his native country. Some attacked him in print, accusing him of being politically naïve. His accusers were wrong. Ondaatje was well aware of the political realities of Sri Lanka. Long before he wrote *Running in the Family*, he published an article entitled "Every Prospect Pleases: Island Ceylon," in which he discussed Roloff Beny's photographic portrait of Ceylon, *To Everything There Is a Season*. He took the photographer to task for misrepresenting Sri Lanka as an Edenic foreign land. Ondaatje's protest was blunt and unforgiving. He maintained that, just the previous year, "the Ceylon government, aided by U.S. helicopters, hunted out rebels by sweeping in and out of the very ruins Beny has peacefully photographed for us." Not one of Beny's photographs showed the carnage, the corpses, the bullet holes — it seemed that only sun and rain, not machine guns, had scarred the statues of Ceylon.

Now that Ondaatje was charged with similar ignorance and insensitivity, he could defend himself only by explaining that his book had been intended to capture the essence of a particular family at a particular time. *Running in the Family* was never meant to be read as either a travelogue or a history of Ceylon. It was a portrait of a wasted, offbeat generation of aristocrats he had never known. Ondaatje asserted that he had returned to his homeland before the fighting between the Tamils and the Sinhalese had broken out, and that he fully realized the country he described was neither the former Ceylon nor the present Sri Lanka. Even in the late 1960s, during conversations with his much more politically committed friend Stuart MacKinnon, Ondaatje eagerly discussed the social unrest that continued to plague Ceylon. Remarks MacKinnon, "Michael was aware of the bloodbath, and of the poets living at the time in Sri Lanka."

With the publication of *Running in the Family*, Ondaatje found himself being labelled an "ethnic writer," albeit one who was politically naïve and overly concerned with aesthetics. His only recourse was to defend himself. He told Hutcheon:

As a writer I don't think I'm concerned with art and aesthetic issues, any more than I would want to be just concerned with making the subject of being a Sri Lankan in Canada my one and only subject. I go to writing to discover as many aspects of myself and the world around me as I can. I go to discover, to explore, not to state the case I already know.

The expectations of the critics who were trying to categorize him were beginning to rankle. Just as they had accused him of being Americanized because he had written about Billy the Kid and Buddy Bolden, they now claimed that he was imposing his aesthetic concerns on ethnicity. Before such charges were ever levelled, however, Ondaatje had spoken out against this simplistic mind-set; if it should become a trend, it would fetter all Canadian writers. To Solecki (in 1984), he remarked that

For writers in Canada today, there's so much stuff being written about them that it's almost like being surrounded and locked up. There is that tendency for critics to try to nail writers down within a literary tradition. But really who cares? A true literary tradition has nothing to do with 1850 to 1980. It's not a line like that.

Not only is it "not a line like that," but also, as Ondaatje told Hutcheon, the author, and no one else, has the right to select his or her own topic: ". . . I like being a writer because of the freedom that is allowed me: I can write about whatever I want to write about." As for the notion that literature has to be direct, moral, and socially correct, he admitted feeling "little responsibility to that sort of demand."

Throughout his career, Ondaatje had stressed that literature was constructed, like a chair, but that a writer, if he or she chooses to do so, could also make literature into a powerful

FIGURE 22

Michael Ondaatje in 1992.

political tool. Ondaatje, himself, had simply elected not to take that second step in any of his major works. In some shorter works, though, he made a number of his political views clear, demonstrating that if he wanted to he could write socially engaged literature. In 1968, for a collection edited by Al Purdy entitled *The New Romans: Candid Canadian Opinions of the U.S.* (designed to criticize American imperialism), Ondaatje did write as powerful a political poem as anyone could ask for. It is called "Pictures from Vietnam," and it is a scathing description of the atrocities that occurred during the Vietnam War. The poem ends: "She laid down the child / skull drained of liquid / its side unlaced like tennis shoes."

RECLAIMING A NEGLECTED HISTORY

Ondaatje has never been inconsistent. He has repeatedly asked readers to consider his works, not his opinions. Still, he has views, and they are strong. And with increasing demands upon him to be socially responsible, he has elucidated his political stand, especially in his most recent novels, *In the Skin of a Lion* (1987) and *The English Patient* (1992). Neither demands to be read as a political statement, though both can be read as bearing one. *In the Skin of a Lion* depicts the experience of those minorities who helped build this country. Most Canadian histories have erased the record of their contribution, but Ondaatje has acted to resurrect it. He has said, and was quoted by Barbara Turner, that "Canada has always been a very racist society. . . ." To highlight that point, he even considered calling the novel "Available Light" (see Butterfield), just to emphasize that what is revealed about a crucial subject (the building of Canada or, at least, the building of its most important and recognizable landmarks) depends upon who is (and who isn't) throwing light on it.

Ondaatje had begun the first sketches for *In the Skin of a Lion* in 1980. He and a friend from his London days, the sculptor

Robert Fones, were driving along Toronto's Don Valley Parkway when Fones mentioned how historically and architecturally interesting the viaduct was. The notion caught Ondaatje's attention. He explained to interviewer Cary Fagan, "I had driven under it about eight hundred times. And so I looked at it and thought, it is a beautiful place." At about that time, Kim Ondaatje was researching Raymond Moriyama, the Toronto architect who built the Ontario Science Centre and Scarborough City Hall ("the only nice thing," Pulver quotes Kim as saying, "about Scarborough"). Soon both Michael and Kim had developed a strong interest in the architects of Toronto. While Moriyama inspired her, Ambrose Small (financier of the Bloor Street Viaduct) and R.C. Harris (designer of the Toronto water-treatment plant) inspired him.

Michael's first effort to explore the material developed into a two-hundred-page manuscript on Ambrose Small, who was known, reports Turner, as " 'the jackal of Toronto's business world,' a millionaire whose disappearance in 1919 occasioned the most vigorous man-hunt in Canadian history." That Michael would even consider choosing such a subject came as a surprise to Christopher. In the end, however, Michael turned away from the initial subject of the novel. Martha Butterfield quotes Christopher:

> Michael didn't really like [Ambrose Small] at all and didn't particularly want to write about him. From being the central character at first Small's role diminished and diminished. Michael gets close to the financial scene but then shies off — unlike me — from "that other world." But then Michael never really understood Ambrose Small.

After Michael had completed a rather sizable manuscript on Small, he recalls, "I began to dislike him intensely, and I became much more interested in the minor characters" (see Turner). These of course, were the Macedonians, who shared his own immigrant background, experience, and sensibility. When this switch occurred is unclear, but while writing the final draft of *In the Skin of a Lion* he was fuelled by a quiet determination to be more conscious of sociological factors than he had ever been before. Like many immigrants, he became indignant at the tendency of Canadian histories to obliterate the memory of, quotes Turner, "the people who actually built the god-damn bridge."

Ondaatje, however, was adamant that, after *Running in the Family*, he did not want to write an "ethnic" book that could — and probably would — be interpreted as his "immigrant" novel. He was also determined not to be seen as a thesis-ridden political writer. Years earlier (in 1984), he had confided to Solecki that "It's a funny thing, political theses I find impossible to read. I have to be affected emotionally or in a sensual way before something hits me." Writing *In the Skin of a Lion*, he still held firmly to this view. At the same time, though, he wanted to suggest what a writer's political role should be. For him, political writing was a matter of imaginatively reclaiming, without lapsing into moralism or didacticism, those events in Canadian history that were often ignored, overlooked, or slanted. Speaking to interviewer Catherine Bush, Ondaatje elaborated:

> I think reclaiming untold stories is an essential role for the writer. Especially in this country, where one can no longer trust the media. The newspapers have such power over the story and portrait of Canada. You can see the newspapers moving in a certain politically right-wing or economically right-wing direction, and this — before you know it — becomes the official voice of the country, the equivalent of a Canadian pavilion at Disneyland. But we know it's not a real truth. One of the things a novel can do is represent the unofficial story. . . .

Ondaatje likes to retreat to his cottage each summer to write. He is still committed to keeping his private life private. Although he is now more vocal about the responsibilities of the writer, he primarily reveals his political views indirectly, and usually only through fiction. The very choice of the name Caravaggio for one of the major characters in both *In the Skin of a Lion* and *The English Patient* is an example of the most direct form of indirect expression that Ondaatje uses. The Italian painter rejected the idealization of any subject in art, and wanted to be recognized for his work, not his personality. He did, nevertheless, become known for his scandalous and lawless ways. Caravaggio represents Ondaatje's consistent view that art, divorced from its maker, must reveal all that it is capable of revealing.

Awards for his "immigrant novel," *In the Skin of a Lion*, and his other contributions to Canadian writing, were showered upon Ondaatje between 1987 and 1988. He won the Toronto Book Award prize of five thousand dollars, and received the Toronto Arts Award for his writing. He shared the stage the evening the latter award was presented with Northrop Frye, who was honoured with a lifetime-achievement award. Frye gave a speech; Ondaatje, as usual, said "Thank you." Ondaatje was also granted the ten-thousand-dollar Trillium Book Award for *In the Skin of a Lion*. The novel then made him one of the three finalists for the fifty-thousand-dollar Ritz Paris Hemingway Literary Prize (the other finalists were Nadine Gordimer, for *A Sport of Nature*, and Toni Morrison, for *Beloved*). Ondaatje didn't win that competition (in fact no prize was awarded), but he did win the Wang International Festival Prize soon afterwards, donating the cash part of the award ($7,500) to a fund for promising young writers. (The fund memorializes his friend, poet bpNichol, who had recently died of cancer at the age of forty-four.) In addition to the cash award, Ondaatje received Wang desktop-publishing equipment valued at fifteen thousand dollars. His jocular comment about the computer, an instrument he is banned from using at Coach House Press because he once erased an entire manuscript with one keystroke, was (as quoted by H.J. Kirchhoff): "I think giving this computer to the last Luddite is ridiculous. . . . It's like giving a Porsche to someone who has just discovered the bicycle." (Ondaatje was actually overjoyed with the prize because it could be used to improve operations at *Brick*, the literary journal he coedits with Linda Spalding.) Not yet done with accolades, he was granted the Best Paperback in English Award for the same novel.

Success has brought Ondaatje another very tangible advantage: the time and the freedom to write. Today, most people can only catch a glimpse of him at the occasional official function, in the Glendon College pool (where he swims regularly to keep his weight down), or — as a York University colleague who pleads anonymity has said — "at the local Radio Shack in the computer software section, because he's hardly ever teaching on campus anymore." Success has given him advantages. He has managed, for example, to obtain release time from teaching. Glendon College, he openly acknowledges, "has been terrific in terms of giving me time off and arranging my classes all in one lump so I can write" (see Turner).

AN ENDURING BOND

While Michael Ondaatje's name was gaining popularity in the publishing market, his brother's was losing it. This was largely due to a controversy in which Christopher had become embroiled. Don Gillmor, writing about the controversy for *Saturday Night*, claims that Christopher had heard from Michael that the publishing firm Lester & Orpen Dennys, in financial straights, was looking for a buyer. Christopher, writes Gillmor (quoting Malcolm Lester), "had had enough of the world of corporate finance, the world of Bay Street, and he wanted to return to his publishing roots."

In the summer of 1988 a deal was struck, and Christopher became chairman of Lester & Orpen Dennys. It was agreed that the firm's previous owners, Malcolm Lester and Louise Dennys, would retain their positions as, respectively, president and publisher. But, as Gillmor reports, almost immediately "The sunny bond [between Christopher and the former owners] began to slip away, strained by the pressures of actual ownership." Christopher gradually withdrew from operations at Lester & Orpen Dennys and began to divest himself of various other corporate holdings. In December of 1988, he sold the publishing house to the Hees Corporation, but stayed on as chairman of the firm. He resigned as chairman in November of 1989 and "left for Sri Lanka . . . to search for his roots and those aspects of himself that continued to elude him." It was the beginning of the end for Lester & Orpen Dennys. After a relatively brief struggle to stay afloat under the direction of its new owner, the firm collapsed in January of 1991.

Many blamed Christopher, who had bought and resold the firm within four months, for its demise. Gillmor claims that "upon hearing of the [initial] sale" of Lester & Orpen Dennys to his brother, "Michael had said, 'Why don't you [Christopher] leave them alone.'" Christopher, apparently, had replied that "That is what he planned to do." This exchange may or may not have actually occurred, but it is clear that Michael was less concerned about the supposed actions of his brother than about the failure of another Canadian publisher. He urged the public to consider the implications of the loss of the firm: "Lester & Orpen Dennys provided a unique voice in Canadian publishing . . . and I don't think we will see a house like theirs again. I think it is a warning" (see Gillmor). The warning, without doubt, is directed towards those who refuse to take seriously this problem: Canadian publishing houses are in trouble; even when run by successful financiers they can't seem to make enough money to survive.

Michael's words underscore his deep commitment to Canadian writing. In 1990, when Lester & Orpen Dennys was still up and running, he created an anthology of Canadian short fiction for the firm. It is called *From Ink Lake*, and contains the work of many of the country's finest writers. The anthology reflects Ondaatje's conviction, stated in the book's introduction, that Canadians "must turn to our literature for the truth about ourselves."

At times it was difficult for Michael to share a fraternal bond with a flamboyant, high-profile financier — it has been the fate of Michael and Christopher Ondaatje, as they are public figures, to be perpetually linked in the minds of others. Henry James (the great psychological novelist) and William James (the novel psychiatrist) had a similar fate; their successes and failures, like those of all such well-known brothers, seem to have been constantly entangled. Leon Edel, in his multivolume biography of Henry James, maintains that an understanding of the nature of sibling rivalry is essential if one is to grasp the significance of the James brothers' achievements. One wonders if the same applies to the Ondaatje brothers. Kim Ondaatje insists that it does not. In her view, there is less of a rivalry and more of a "sharing of similar problems." This seems to be substantiated by the fact that Michael and Christopher occasionally work together. When Michael, for example, agreed to coedit a book intended to attract attention to the aims of Amnesty International and to raise funds for that organization, he asked Christopher to lend a hand. The book, entitled *Brushes with Greatness*, was designed as a spoof: it is a collection of short pieces, by various writers, describing their chance encounters with celebrities. Both Ondaatjes had, to a certain extent, weathered the vicissitudes of fame, and so each contributed to the project with a healthy sense of self-ridicule.

AN EPILOGUE IS ONLY A PROLOGUE

In his introduction to *Leonard Cohen*, Ondaatje wrote, "It is impossible to write a biography . . . on someone still halfway through his career without becoming out of date." He is right, of course. Ondaatje's biography might have ended here — as I had planned it to — with an emphasis on *From Ink Lake* and his inestimable contribution to Canada and Canadian writers. But on 13 October 1992, at forty-nine, Ondaatje became the first Canadian to win the prestigious Booker Prize. In one night

FIGURE 23

Booker Prize winner Michael Ondaatje.

Ondaatje's status as an international writer had been confirmed. Novels by Margaret Atwood, Robertson Davies, and Mordecai Richler had been shortlisted in previous years, but had failed to win. Ondaatje garnered the award for his novel *The English Patient*, and everybody wanted to know about him. The mystique of Michael Ondaatje was no longer merely a Canadian affair. American and British reporters and interviewers suddenly discovered the adamantly silent author, and they also discovered that he was not interested in seizing the opportunity to push his own books.

Ondaatje wasn't posing or feigning. International recognition simply wasn't going to change him. Several weeks before the Booker announcement, he had confided to *Books in Canada* reviewer Keith Nickson that, in all likelihood, British novelist Barry Unsworth would win the Booker for a novel entitled *Sacred Hunger*. Ondaatje had already read the book, and with his sharp eye for literary talent recognized its merits. He wasn't far wrong in his evaluation of Unsworth's skills; indeed, he was surprised that the final result was a tie. Ondaatje would share both first place and the award of twenty thousand pounds (roughly forty-five thousand Canadian dollars). "[T]he television cameras," reported Maureen Garvie, "picked up genuine astonishment on the writer's face as his name was read out." Compelled to speak on British national television, Ondaatje claimed to have only "20 seconds" to accept the award, graciously thanked the Canadian publishing industry, and hastened off stage.

Ondaatje did not seek the controversy that the tie touched off. It wasn't his fault that the judges couldn't make up their minds. Most American and Canadian reviewers liked the book; only the British press had mixed reactions. They debated about Ondaatje's literary skills, and circulated the rumour that he had received a seventy-thousand-pound royalty advance. That Ondaatje was more nervous about the results than he let on is confirmed by his reaction to Vicky Gabereau when she interviewed him for CBC Radio and mentioned his last-minute decision to rewrite the ending of the book: "How did you find that out?" he blurted.

"You let it slip to one of the British reporters," she answered. "It's all in the papers."

The bookies, of course, had a field day; they treated the whole thing like a horse race, and offered five-to-two odds on Ondaatje. They knew what they were doing. *The English Patient*, which appeared five years after *In the Skin of a Lion*, is an exquisitely rendered account of the interconnected lives of four survivors — the Patient, Hana, Kip, and Caravaggio — who take refuge in an abandoned Tuscan villa in the twilight of World War II. It is filled with the vivid, violent, disturbing images for which Ondaatje has become so well known. At the same time, it is his most personally revealing novel. Its representation of Hana's stepmother canoeing is based on Ondaatje's own canoe trips with friends in Algonquin Park; its description of the Skootamatta River flowing through the Canadian Shield recaptures the scene from his own cottage window. Despite its structural complexities, then, *The English Patient* is, as Douglas Barbour has remarked, "possibly Ondaatje's most accessible fiction. Yet it rejects nothing of the style and intensity of vision that marked his earlier works."

Like Ondaatje's earlier novels, *The English Patient* is the result of his now recognizable and understandable habit of mind. One figure — a gunslinger, falsely mythologized; a cornetist gone insane, retreating into silence; a drunk inexplicably driven to self-destruction — first captures his imagination and then compels him to explore. In a sense, Ondaatje is still looking for the father figure he lost in youth. With *The English Patient*, his mind was seized by a vision of an unnamed man, disfigured, aflame in the desert. He is, in part, the figure that always haunts Ondaatje, the unrecognized, displaced individual who is wrenched out of his home and his environment. The novel tantalizes the reader. The faceless man might be the Count Ladislaus de Almásy, an actual explorer who lived for years in the desert and who really did lose his face and his identity. The man might be British. He might also be a Hungarian or a spy for the Germans or both. The lack of a clear identity, and the need to find one, is one of the main undercurrents of Ondaatje's prose. Just as there is no clear picture of Billy the Kid, there is no recognizable face of the title figure of *The English Patient*. In a sense, the novel is the self-portrait of Michael Ondaatje; it contains his archetype of self and his bewilderment about his own uncertain origins — Sri Lanka, England, Canada.

The dominating sense of disruption and dislocation that pervades *The English Patient* did not, of course, go unnoticed by Ondaatje himself. When interviewed by Beverley Slopen for *Publisher's Weekly*, he candidly admitted that his theme was, as he saw it, the common crisis of the immigrants of the twentieth century with whom he identifies: "All those people born in one place who live in another place have lost their source. In a new continent, the past is a shadowy area and the only way they can survive is to deal in the present."

Ondaatje's manner of writing *The English Patient* is typical of his way of dealing "in the present" while searching for the past that gave rise to it. The vision of the burning man in need of healing initiated his investigation. He began to suspect that at the heart of the book was the intimacy between Hana and the English Patient. The love story grew. But then, Ondaatje told Stephen Smith, "suddenly [he snaps his fingers] Kip showed up." From there he turned to the method of composition that has almost always fired his imagination: research. To Val Ross he explained, "As a boy I read books on bombs, and I wanted to be a frogman" in order to dismantle them. As an adult, he could turn to textbooks and technical journals to understand how bombs are made and defused. The Persian Gulf War of 1991, which Ondaatje (and the world) witnessed on television, both horrified and fascinated him, especially when he saw soldiers digging unexploded "bombs out of the sand."

The novel was already well under way when he went to the Royal Geographical Society in London to read detailed descriptions of deserts and their terrains. Also, with the permission of Louise Dennys, Ondaatje read her mother's private correspondence, which described what it was like to be in Egypt during

World War II. *The English Patient*, written and rewritten over a five-year period, took on a more coherent shape after Ondaatje completed a short teaching stint in Rome in 1990. While in Italy, he visited the villa of the Italian poet D'Annunzio, taking detailed notes about its construction and architecture. He eventually drew on that material to enhance the descriptions of the ruined Tuscan villa of *The English Patient*. As he had before, Ondaatje blended emotions and historical information culled from various sources, including novels about the Blitzkrieg and historical accounts of Canadian nursing.

Ross reports that Ondaatje prefers composing with pen in hand. He then cuts and pastes and experiments with the order of the units. To look for word echoes and patterns, he types the drafts into the computer and relies on the search-string key to isolate repeated motifs. As each section takes shape, he reads the material into a tape recorder "to hear the poetry." Thus, much of the cadence and the poetic rhythm of the novel is the result of his determination to have its various static images and scenes linked by nuances of sound and word echo rather than by plot or action. "I don't like to throw my characters into a plot as though it were a raging torrent. . . . What interests me are the complications and nuances of character" (see Slopen).

Once the basic manuscript was finished in 1991, he sent it, as he does all of his manuscripts, to "friends he could trust." He names three editors who were especially involved with close readings of *The English Patient*: Ellen Seligman, at McClelland and Stewart in Toronto; Liz Calder, at Bloomsbury in London; and Sonny Mehta, at Knopf in New York. Mehta, the head of Knopf, responded to the manuscript in considerable detail. All the readers seem to have understood Ondaatje's overriding concern, Slopen suggests when she quotes Ondaatje explaining his sense of the issue:

I didn't want the reader to feel locked into one character. I love that sense that history is not just one opinion. I prefer a complicated history where an event is seen through many eyes or emotions, and the writer doesn't try to control the viewpoint. It is only when one steps back from those small things which are knitted together in the narrative that one can see, as Henry James said, the "figure in the carpet."

It wasn't the need for more action that Ondaatje wanted to hear about from those he trusted. He knew, he said to Stephen Smith of *Quill and Quire,* "right from the beginning that [*The English Patient*] was a very political book — though not from the point of view of a politician or a sociologist — but in [the sense] that it's about the effect on four real humans of this panoramic event."

Although self-consciously absorbed by the inner experiences of his characters and fully aware of other people's overwhelming need to understand the inner, private experience of those who absorb them, he continues to reject the idea that outsiders have the right to infringe upon his inner life. Even his most loyal readers are barred from having a glimpse of the private Ondaatje. Keith Nickson, in an attempt to break through the mask for *Quill and Quire,* asked for a personal interview on tape, and he and Ondaatje "haggled" about what was to be recorded. When Val Ross arranged an interview, Ondaatje laid down the law: a neutral place, no questions about his relationship with Christopher Ondaatje, and no attempts to talk to or about Linda Spalding.

In 1994, Ondaatje is still militant about keeping the world at bay. His letters, manuscripts, and galleys, purchased by the National Archives of Canada, may be viewed only with Ondaatje's written permission. The massive Coach House collection of papers, bought by the same archive, contains virtually no letters, papers, or manuscripts by or about Michael Ondaatje. As far as anyone knows, all such documents were removed before the collection was put up for sale. Even York University officials, I was told (by people who are understandably not named), were specifically asked by Ondaatje to withhold all documents dealing with his teaching career, awards, and years of sabbatical from the public.

Ondaatje — and he has never waivered on this point — has always rejected the cult of the author. He frequently reiterates that he has seen too many writers turned into media images. As he told Ross, the fear of being manipulated into a prepackaged, saleable product is "the cause of all this paranoia."

Now fifty plus, his body thicker, his hair and beard shot with grey, his blue eyes still compelling, he is no longer the charmingly innocent nineteen-year-old immigrant hoping to make a mark. He has, as he expressed it to Linda Hutcheon, remade himself, and he has approached the point in his life where — given his successes as novelist and editor and teacher — he is gradually learning to assume the role of patriarch of his artistic community. He doesn't shrug off this role. When, in 1992, he was honoured by the Canada Council with another Governor General's Award (this time for *The English Patient*), he surprised everyone. Instead of mumbling a few words of thanks as he had done at previous ceremonies, he lambasted the Tory government. The speech was a prepared one, and he allowed the text to be published in the Montreal *Gazette* under the headline "Worth Quoting: Author Delivers Stinging Attack on the GST." Ondaatje made it clear that he felt Mulroney's policy of imposing a tax on books was absolutely dangerous to "literature and literacy." Canadian art and culture were at stake; he had to speak out. The normally staid event, staged to remind people that the arts are supported by the Canadian government, instantly became a forum for debate. Years earlier, when Ondaatje was denied a job at the University of Western Ontario, he refused to exploit his Governor General's Award to lend weight to personal expressions, but now that he considered Canadian culture to be threatened, he didn't hesitate. His action suggests that he will wear well the mantle of international recognition bestowed upon him as the first Canadian author to win the Booker Prize.

It was Kim Ondaatje who caught what is perhaps the most revealing moment of Michael Ondaatje's artistic career in Canada in a photograph. One day, just after Ondaatje had won his first Governor General's Award — and at a time when he was faced with the loss of his job at Western and was wondering about what really constituted a writer's responsibility and whether he should speak his mind publicly — Kim noticed that they were standing beside a billboard that seemed to get at the heart of the matter. She couldn't resist photographing Michael standing beneath the billboard, which reads "Express yourself beautifully." Like all pictures — and like all honest biographies — it says everything without saying anything. Kim had always hoped to transform the photo into a painting, but she could never get the lettering right. Michael, of course, then — as now — refuses comment.

CHRONOLOGY

1943   Philip Michael Ondaatje is born on 12 September to Mervyn and Doris Ondaatje on a tea estate in Kegalle, Ceylon (now Sri Lanka), the fourth of four children.

1945   Michael Ondaatje's parents divorce; his mother moves with her children to Colombo, Sri Lanka.

1949–52   Ondaatje attends Saint Thomas's College Boys' School, Colombo, Sri Lanka.

1952–62   The family moves to England, and Ondaatje attends Dulwich College, London.

1962   Ondaatje immigrates to Canada.

1962–64   In Lennoxville, Quebec, he attends Bishop's University, and wins the President's Prize for English. He marries Betty Jane Kimbark (Kim Jones) in 1964. Their first child, a daughter, Quintin Ondaatje, is born.

1964–65   Ondaatje transfers to University College, University of Toronto. In 1965, he receives a B.A. degree and is given the Ralph Gustafson Award. He enters the M.A. program at Queen's University in Kingston.

1966   His poems are included in a major anthology, *New Wave Canada*, edited by Raymond Souster. He ties for the E.J. Pratt Gold Medal for Poetry, and wins the Norma Epstein Award for Poetry.

1967   He completes his M.A. degree at Queen's University, and publishes his first book, *The Dainty Monsters*. A second child, Griffin, is born. Ondaatje begins teaching at the University of Western Ontario in London, and is awarded that institution's President's Medal for the poem "Paris."

1968	*The Man with Seven Toes* is performed at the Vancouver Festival.
1969	*The Man with Seven Toes* is published.
1970–71	*The Collected Works of Billy the Kid: Left Handed Poems* is published, as is Ondaatje's study, *Leonard Cohen*, for McClelland and Stewart's Canadian Writers Series. His film *Sons of Captain Poetry* is released, and he works as an editor for Coach House Press. *Billy the Kid* wins the Governor General's Award.
1971	Ondaatje is fired from his job at the University of Western Ontario, and is hired by the Glendon College Department of English, York University. *The Broken Ark: A Book of Beasts* is published.
1972	Ondaatje works on two films. He completes the comic short *Carry on Crime and Punishment* and, from 1972 to 1973, shoots the documentary *The Clinton Special*.
1973	*Rat Jelly* is published. The play of *The Collected Works of Billy the Kid* is produced at the Stratford Festival. *The Collected Works of Billy the Kid: Left Handed Poems* wins the Chalmers Award.
1974	*The Clinton Special* is released.
1976	*Coming through Slaughter* appears, and is cowinner of the *Books in Canada* First Novel Award.
1977	Ondaatje edits *Personal Fictions: Stories by Munro, Wiebe, Thomas, and Blaise*.
1978	*Elimination Dance* is published.
1979	*There's a Trick with a Knife I'm Learning to Do* is published. Ondaatje edits *The Long Poem Anthology*, and wins the du Maurier Award for Poetry.
1980	He wins the Governor General's Award and the Canadian Authors Association Award for *There's a Trick with a Knife I'm Learning to Do*. The play *Coming through Slaughter* is produced at Theatre Passe Muraille in Toronto. He receives the Canada-Australia Literary Prize.
1981	Ondaatje is a visiting professor at the University of

Hawaii at Manoa. He meets Linda Spalding, and separates from Kim Ondaatje.

1982   *Running in the Family* and *Tin Roof* are both published. Ondaatje resumes teaching in the Glendon College English department. He takes first prize in the short-story category of CBC Radio's Annual Literary Competition for "The Passions of Lalla."

1984   *Secular Love* appears.

1985   Ondaatje serves as contributing editor of *Brick*.

1987–88   *In the Skin of a Lion* is published in 1987 and receives the City of Toronto Book Award. Ondaatje also wins the Trillium Book Award; is a finalist for the Ritz Paris Hemingway Award (no award is given); receives the Wang Festival of Arts Award (and donates $7,500, the cash portion of the award, to the bpNichol Fund for Promising Young Writers); wins the Best Paperback in English Award; and, in 1988, receives the Order of Canada.

1989   *The Cinnamon Peeler: Selected Poems* is published in Great Britain.

1990   *From Ink Lake: Canadian Stories Selected by Michael Ondaatje* appears. Ondaatje is visiting professor at Brown University in Providence, Rhode Island.

1991   *The Cinnamon Peeler: Selected Poems* is published in the United States. Ondaatje coedits *The Brick Reader* with Linda Spalding.

1992   *The Cinnamon Peeler: Selected Poems* is published in Canada. *The English Patient* appears, and receives the Booker Prize, the Governor General's Award, and the Trillium Award.

WORKS CONSULTED

Abley, Mark. "Home Is Where the Hurt Is." *Maclean's* 23 Apr. 1979: 62.

Adachi, Ken. "Startling Perception Yields Secrets Sparingly." Rev. of *Secular Love*, by Michael Ondaatje; and *The Whole Night, Coming Home*, by Roo Borson. *Toronto Star* 24 Nov. 1984: M4.

"Award-Winning London Author Appointed to York Teaching Post." *London Free Press* 19 May 1971: 2.

Barbour, Douglas. *Michael Ondaatje*. Twayne's World Authors Series: Canadian Literature 835. New York: Twayne–Macmillan, 1993.

Bryant, Darrol. Letter to the author. 15 Feb. 1994.

Butterfield, Martha. "The One Lighted Room: *In the Skin of a Lion*." *Canadian Literature* 119 (1988): 162–67.

"The Charm of Kingston." *CBC Tuesday Night*. CBC Radio. 11 Dec. 1973.

Clifford, Wayne. Personal Interview. 3 Dec. 1993.

Currie, Bob. "Writer Wins $10,000 Award for Labor Saga." *Vancouver Sun* 12 May 1988: E4.

De Silva, C.R. "Education." *Sri Lanka: A Survey*. Ed. K.M. De Silva. London: Hurst, 1977. 403–33.

"Diefenbaker Raps Poet." *London Free Press* 30 Nov. 1971: 27.

Dragland, Stan. Written comments to the author on a draft of "Michael Ondaatje: Express Yourself Beautifully." 14 Feb. 1992.

Dudek, Louis. "Poetry for the Sixties." *Selected Essays and Criticism*. Ottawa: Tecumseh, 1978. 269–81.

Enright, Robert. "Poetry Notes." *CV/II* Aug. 1976: 3.

Evans, Ron. Interview with Ron Evans. With Robert Fulford. *This Is Robert Fulford*. CBC Radio. 9 Dec. 1972.

Freedman, Adele. "From Gunslingers to Jazz Musicians." *Globe and Mail* 22 Dec. 1979: E1.

Gallager, Noel. "Ondaatje Still Part of London Literary Community." *London Free Press* 6 Apr. 1979: D6.

Garvie, Maureen. "Listening to Michael Ondaatje." *Queen's Quarterly* 99 (1992): 928–34.

Gefen, Pearl Sheffy. "If I Were 19 Now, I'd Maybe Be a Filmmaker." *Globe and Mail* 4 May 1990: D3.

Gillan, Thomas. " 'Pot Shot at Book Was Way Off the Mark.' " Letter. *Toronto Star* 7 Dec. 1971: 7.

Gillmor, Don. "Dangerous Liaisons." *Saturday Night* Sept. 1991: 14–17, 58.

Harris, J.A. Rev. of *Made in Canada: New Poems of the Seventies*, ed. Douglas Lochhead and Raymond Souster; and *Soundings: New Canadian Poets*, ed. Jack Ludwig and Andy Wainwright. *Canadian Forum* June 1971: 38.

Jayaweera, Swarna. "Education." *Modern Sri Lanka: A Society in Transition.* Ed. Tissa Fernando and Robert N. Kearney. Foreign and Comparative Studies, South Asian Series 4. [Syracuse:] Maxwell School of Citizenship and Public Affairs, Syracuse University, 1979. 129–51.

Karedo, Urjo. "An Immigrant's Song." *Saturday Night* Dec. 1983: 44–51.

Kirchhoff, H.J. " 'The Last Luddite' Collects Another Literary Honour." *Globe and Mail* 24 Oct. 1988: C7.

Layton, Irving. "Anglo-Canadian." *Collected Poems.* Toronto: McClelland, 1971. 151.

McClelland, Joe. "Ondaatje to Leave Western: Won't Seek Doctorate, Honored Writer Loses Job." *London Free Press* 8 Mar. 1971: 3.

MacKinnon, Stuart. Personal Interview. 15 Aug. 1992.

Mandel, Ann. "Michael Ondaatje (12 September 1943–)." *Canadian Writers Since 1960. Dictionary of Literary Biography.* 2nd ser. 1987.

Mandel, Eli. Interview with Eli Mandel. With Peter Gzowski. *This Country in the Morning.* CBC Radio. 17 June 1974.

Marshall, Tom. "Literary Kingston." *Cross-Canada Writer's Quarterly* 8.3 (1986): 21–23.

"Michael Ondaatje and the UWO." Editorial. *London Free Press* 11 Mar. 1971: 8.

Mundwiler, Leslie. *Michael Ondaatje: Word, Image, Imagination.* New Canadian Criticism Series. Vancouver: Talonbooks, 1984.

Nichol, bp. [Notes on contributors.] *The Cosmic Chef Glee and Perloo Memorial Society under the Direction of Captain Poetry Presents — an*

Evening of Concrete. Ed. Nichol. Ottawa: Oberon, 1970.

Nickson, Keith. "The Ondaatje Mystique." *Books in Canada* Dec. 1992: 6.

Ondaatje, Christopher. *The Man-Eater of Punanai: A Journey of Discovery to the Jungles of Old Ceylon.* Toronto: Harper, 1992.

Ondaatje, Kim. Personal Interview. 23–25 Oct. 1992.

Ondaatje, Michael. *The Broken Ark: A Book of Beasts.* Ottawa: Oberon, 1971.

——. *The Collected Works of Billy the Kid: Left Handed Poems.* Toronto: Anansi, 1970.

——. *Coming through Slaughter.* Anansi Fiction 36. Toronto: Anansi, 1976.

——. "A Conversation with Michael Ondaatje." With Stephen Scobie and Douglas Barbour. *White Pelican* 1.2 (1971): 6–15.

——. *The Dainty Monsters.* Toronto: Coach House, 1967.

——. "Every Prospect Pleases: Island Ceylon." *Books in Canada* Dec. 1971: 17–19.

——. *From Ink Lake: Canadian Stories Selected by Michael Ondaatje.* Toronto: Lester, 1990.

——. Interview with Michael Ondaatje. With Vicky Gabereau. CBC Radio. 12 Oct. 1993.

——. "An Interview with Michael Ondaatje (1975)." With Sam Solecki. Solecki 13–27.

——. "An Interview with Michael Ondaatje (1984)." With Sam Solecki. Solecki 321–32.

——. Interview (by mail) with an anonymous correspondent. *Manna* 1 (1972): 19–22.

——. "In the Skin of the Patient: Michael Ondaatje on the Structure, Intimacy, and Politics of His New Novel." With Stephen Smith. *Quill and Quire* Sept. 1992: 69.

——. *Leonard Cohen.* Canadian Writers Series 5. Toronto: McClelland, 1970.

——. Letter to the Author. 23 May 1991.

——. Letter to Michael Moore. 1 Feb. 1988.

——. "Little Magazines/Small Presses 1969." *artscanada* Aug. 1969: 17–18.

——. "Michael Ondaatje: An Interview." With Catherine Bush. *Conjunctions* 15 (1990): 87–98.

———. "Michael Ondaatje: Interview by Linda Hutcheon." *Other Solitudes: Canadian Multicultural Fictions.* Ed. Hutcheon and Marion Richmond. Toronto: Oxford UP, 1990. 196–202.

———. "Michael Ondaatje [George Whalley: Remembrances]." *George Whalley: Remembrances.* Ed. Michael D. Moore. Kingston: Quarry, 1989. 120–24.

———. "Moving to the Clear: Michael Ondaatje." With Jon Pearce. *Twelve Voices: Interviews with Canadian Poets.* Ed. Pearce. Ottawa: Borealis, 1980. 131–43.

———. "Mythology in the Poetry of Edwin Muir: A Study of the Making and the Using of Mythology in Edwin Muir's Poetry." M.A. thesis. Queen's U, 1967.

———. "Peter." *How Do I Love Thee: Sixty Poets of Canada (and Quebec) Select and Introduce Their Favourite Poems from Their Own Work.* Ed. John Robert Colombo. Edmonton: Hurtig, 1970. 145–49.

———. "Pictures from Vietnam." *The New Romans: Candid Canadian Opinions of the U.S.* Ed. Al Purdy. Edmonton: Hurtig [1968]. 131.

———. *Rat Jelly.* Toronto: Coach House, 1973.

———. "Roy Kiyooka." *artscanada* Oct.–Nov. 1968: 45.

———. *Running in the Family.* Toronto: McClelland, 1982.

———. *There's a Trick with a Knife I'm Learning to Do: Poems 1963–1978.* New York: Norton, 1979.

———. "Where the Personal and the Historical Meet: An Interview with Michael Ondaatje." With Cary Fagan. *Paragraph: The Canadian Fiction Review* 12.2 (1990): 3–5.

———. "Worth Quoting: Author Delivers Stinging Attack on the GST." *Gazette* [Montreal] 5 Dec. 1992: B6.

———. "Writer Clarifies Departure from Western Teaching Post." Letter. *London Free Press* 13 Mar. 1971: 6.

"Ondaatje, Michael. 1943– ." *Contemporary Authors.* 1974.

"Ondaatje, Philip Michael." *The Canadian Who's Who.* 1972.

"Ondaatje Says He'll Refuse Study Bursary." *London Free Press* 20 Apr. 1971: 3.

"Ondaatje Wins Literary Prize." *Globe and Mail* 26 July 1980: E9.

"Pinnacles of Success (CAA Literary Awards)." *Canadian Author and Bookman* 55–56 (1980): 12–13.

Pulver, David. "Diary of a Bittersweet Experience." *Whig-Standard Magazine* 9 Aug. 1980: 18.

Quill, Greg. "Toronto Honors the Best with Annual Awards." *Toronto Star* 23 Sept. 1987: F1.

Rodriguez, Elizabeth. "A Report on the Poets at Festival 70 (Bishop's University)." *Fiddlehead* Mar.–Apr. 1970: 124–25.

Rosenblatt, Joe. Letter to the author. 15 Oct. 1993.

Ross, Val. "Minefields of the Mind." *Globe and Mail* 10 Oct. 1992: C1, C6.

Siblin, Eric. "Literary Winner Ondaatje Blasts Tory Government." *Kitchener-Waterloo Record* 1 Dec. 1992: C5.

Slopen, Beverley. "Michael Ondaatje." *Publishers Weekly* 5 Oct. 1992: 48–49.

Solecki, Sam, ed. *Spider Blues: Essays on Michael Ondaatje*. Ed. Solecki. Montreal: Véhicule, 1985.

Souster, Raymond, ed. *New Wave Canada: The New Explosion in Canadian Poetry*. Toronto: Contact, 1966.

"Speaking Play." *QUAD* (1964): 90.

Turner, Barbara. "In the Skin of Michael Ondaatje: Giving Voice to a Social Conscience." *Quill and Quire* May 1987: 21–22.

Urquhart, Tony. Telephone Interview. 22 Dec. 1993.

Whalley, Elizabeth. Personal Interview. 23–25 Oct. 1992.

Whittaker, Herbert. "A Poet's Bid to Undo His Own Bandit." *Globe and Mail* 25 Oct. 1974: 13.

Witten, Mark. "Billy, Buddy, and Michael: The Collected Writings of Michael Ondaatje Are a Composite Portrait of the Artist as a Private 'I.' " *Books in Canada* June–July 1977: 9–10, 12–13.

——— . "The Case of the Midwife Lode." *Books in Canada* Dec. 1977: 6–8.

Woods, Elizabeth. "Poet's Progress." *Quill and Quire* June 1979: 28.